KV-578-258

Rex and Thea Rienits

Discovery of

Australia

illustrated by
Harry and Gwen Green

Hamlyn - London
Sun Books - Melbourne

FOREWORD

Geologically Australia is the world's oldest continent. Historically it is the youngest. For centuries scholars had talked about an unknown south land, but they had no idea where it was or how big it was, and most of their guesses were wild and wide of the mark. Europeans may have visited Australia in the sixteenth century but if so they left no record; and the earliest authenticated visitors were the Dutch who at intervals during the seventeenth century sighted, examined and charted much of its north, west and south coasts. What they saw impressed them so little, however, that they saw neither point nor profit in colonising it, and for almost another century it remained the continent nobody wanted. Then in 1770 Cook discovered and explored its fertile east coast. Eighteen years later the first English settlement was founded on the shores of Sydney Cove, and Australian history had begun. It has been a quiet history. No major revolutions have been fought on its soil; it has known no invaders, and until World War II it had never been threatened by invasion. Yet this youngest of the nations has not lacked heroes – men and women who have devoted their lives to it and not infrequently died for it. This story is about them.

Published by The Hamlyn Publishing Group Ltd
London · New York · Sydney · Toronto
Hamlyn House, Feltham, Middlesex, England
In association with Sun Books Pty. Ltd. Melbourne.

Copyright © 1969 by The Hamlyn Publishing Group Ltd

ISBN 0 600 00280 2

Photoset by BAS Printers Limited, Wallop, Hampshire
Colour separations by Schwitter Limited, Zurich
Printed in Holland by Smeets, Weert

CONTENTS

In the beginning

The discoverers of Australia were, of course, the Aborigines. They were of two races and they came from the north in waves, the first probably about 20,000 years ago. There are theories but no certainty regarding the place of origin of these peoples. The first, whom anthropologists call Tasmanoids, may have come from New Guinea or other Melanesian islands; the second, known as Australoids, were probably from southern India. Although racially unalike, similarities in their way of life and some customs suggest there was some intermingling between them. Generally, however, it is thought they were enemies and that eventually the Tasmanoids were driven to the south-east corner when Tasmania was still either part of the mainland or close enough to be reached in canoes. Here they remained until the coming of the white man two centuries ago. In another century they were extinct. The mainland Aborigines, were hunted like animals, their Stone Age weapons no match for the invaders' firearms. Debased by liquor and weakened by white men's diseases, they seemed likely for awhile to suffer the same fate.

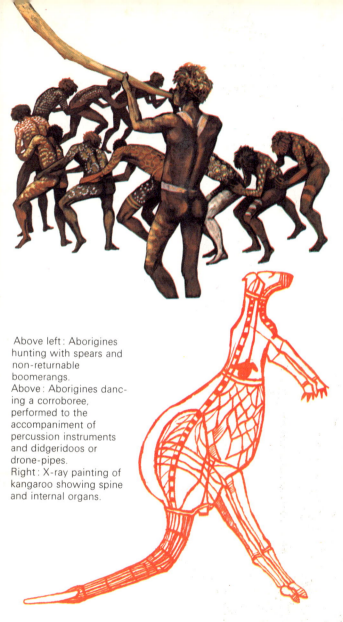

Above left: Aborigines
hunting with spears and
non-returnable
boomerangs.
Above: Aborigines danc-
ing a corroboree,
performed to the
accompaniment of
percussion instruments
and didgeridoos or
drone-pipes.
Right: X-ray painting of
kangaroo showing spine
and internal organs.

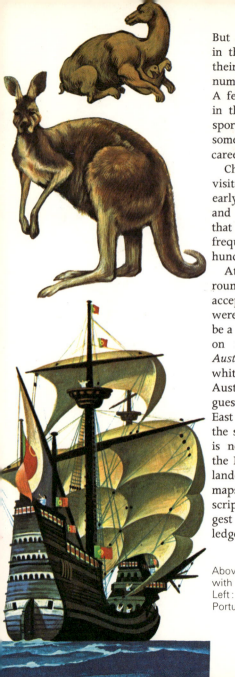

But a more humane attitude in this century has stopped their decimation, and their numbers are now increasing. A few have even won fame in the fields of culture and sport, and there are already some who seek political careers.

Chinese junks may have visited northern Australia as early as the fifteenth century, and there is ample evidence that Malayan fishermen were frequent visitors for some hundreds of years.

At this time when the roundness of the world was accepted as a fact, old theories were revived that there must be a great southern continent on its underside – *Terra Australis Incognita*. The first white men to come near Australia were the Portuguese, who dominated the East Indies through most of the sixteenth century. There is no certain evidence that the Portuguese ever actually landed on the continent, but maps and geographical descriptions of the period suggest they had some knowledge of it, and an engraving

Above: a kangaroo compared with a fanciful version of 1597. Left: a sixteenth-century Portuguese carrack.

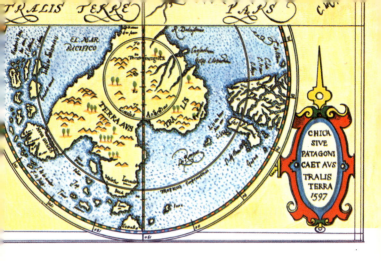

Wytfliet's map which shows Australia and New Guinea separated by the strait named after the Spanish explorer Torres.

of an animal vaguely like a kangaroo, published in 1597, supports this possibility.

The first two Englishmen to sail around the world – Francis Drake (between 1577 and 1580) and Thomas Cavendish (1586–1588) – went north of Australia and missed it by some hundreds of miles. So did two Spanish navigators who crossed the Pacific in search of a southern continent which geographers said must exist to balance the land mass of the northern hemisphere. These were Alvara de Mendaña, who discovered the Solomon Islands in 1568, and Pedro de Quirós, who reached the New Hebrides, 1200 miles east of Australia, in 1605. De Quirós made sure he had found the new continent and named it Austrialia del Espiritu Santo. But his lieutenant, Luis Vaez de Torres, was sure it was only an island, and he was right. Today it is called simply Santo. Torres left de Quirós, sailed on to the west, and in July and August 1606 passed through Torres Strait, which separates Australia and New Guinea. It is doubtful whether he actually saw the Australian mainland, but it is not important, for a Dutchman, Willem Jansz, had already done so, and landed on it, three months before.

7

The Dutch

The Dutch had increased their maritime power so greatly in the late sixteenth century that by 1606 they had supplanted the Portuguese as masters of the East Indies. They had occupied the Cape of Good Hope, commanding the approach to the Indies; they had formed a military and trading base at Batavia, now Jakarta; they had conquered the rich Spice Islands; and their ships ranged as far as Japan.

The Dutch were interested in new lands only for the raw materials they might produce. Early in 1606 Willem Jansz was sent from Bantam, Java, in the yacht *Duyfken* to see what the south coast of New Guinea offered. From here he sailed south-west, missing Torres Strait, and found himself off the western coast of what is now Cape York peninsula. It was barren and unpromising, and at a point he called Keer-Weer (Cape Turnagain) he turned for home. At the estuary of the present Wenlock River the crew of a boat sent ashore for water were attacked by Aborigines and one was killed. This

Hendrick Brouwer, famous Dutch captain, against a background of Dutch shipping at Amsterdam.

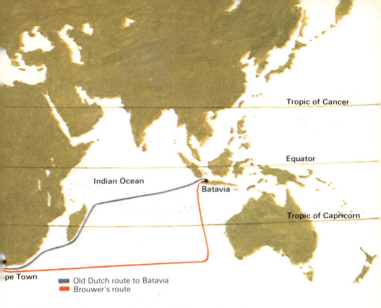

Original Dutch route to the East Indies and the faster one, due east and then north, pioneered by Brouwer.

and Jansz's poor report on the land he had seen, effectively discouraged Dutch interest in the area for some years.

The usual route to the East Indies, north-east from the Cape of Good Hope, brought ships into the doldrums of the Indian Ocean, where they were often becalmed for many weeks. In 1611 a captain named Hendrik Brouwer avoided this by sailing east for about 3,000 miles from the Cape, then north for Batavia. With helpful winds and currents he made record time, which so impressed the Dutch East India Company that they ordered all captains to take the same route.

As the Cape of Good Hope and the west coast of Australia are in the same latitude and only about 4,300 miles apart, it was inevitable that other captains would eventually reach it. The first was Dirk Hartog in the *Eendracht* in October 1616. After examining about 250 miles of coastline Hartog landed on an island which still bears his name and left an inscribed pewter plate recording his visit. He named the part of the mainland he had seen Eendracht Land. When news of the

9

discovery reached Holland it was thought this new country might be identical with Beach, a land rich in gold and spices which the traveller Marco Polo had reported as existing in the south, and captains were ordered to look out for it. Even before this, however, other Dutch ships had seen the Australian coast, among them the *Zeewolf* and *Mauritius*, both in 1618 in the vicinity of the present Point Cloates and Exmouth Gulf.

In July 1619 two ships commanded by Frederik de Houtman reached the coast south of Eendracht Land near the Swan River. Houtman mistook Rottnest Island for a cape, failed to see the river beyond it, and two days later on his way north encountered a dangerous cluster of reefs and small islands which he named the Abrolhos, a Portuguese word of warning to keep one's eyes open. He called the coastline he had found Edel Land after his supercargo, Jacob d'Edel. Three years later the *Leeuwin* came in sight of the coast at its extreme south-western point, and gave its name to Cape Leeuwin and Leeuwin Land.

Other discoveries followed. In 1623 Jan Carstenz sailed from Java and found the present Arnhem Land, which he named after one of his yachts. The following year the *Gulden Zeepeard* made landfall near Cape Leeuwin and sailed eastward for about 1,000 miles to some islands at the head of the Great Australian Bight. The islands and the mainland coast were both named after Pieter Nuyts, an important official who was on board. Two years later the *Vyanen* examined about 200 miles of the coastline north-east of Exmouth Gulf, which the captain Gerrit de Witt named after himself. By now the coastline was well if still imperfectly known, and a fairly clear picture of more than 2,500 miles of it had emerged.

Occasional wrecks were inevitable. The best-known of these is that of the *Batavia* which was lost on Houtman's Abrolhos in 1629. Those aboard managed to get ashore on a small island, and the captain, Francis Pelsart, left in an open

Francis Pelsart hanged the mutineers who had murdered some survivors of his ship, the *Batavia*, after she had been wrecked on Houtman's Abrolhos.

boat to bring help from Batavia. In his absence some of the crew mutinied and murdered 125 passengers and others who opposed them. Forewarned on his return, Pelsart captured the mutineers, hanged some, including the ringleader, Jeronimus Cornelisz, and marooned two on the mainland.

Anthony van Diemen, who became governor-general of the Dutch East Indies in 1636, wanted to know more about New Holland, as the country to the south was now known, and also to find a practical sea-route to South America. With these objects in view two ships, the *Heemskerck* and *Zeehaen*, commanded by Abel Janszoon Tasman, left Batavia in 1642. After a call at Mauritius for stores Tasman sailed south and then east till he reached what is now Tasmania. Rounding its southern cape he anchored in Frederick Henry Bay (the present Blackman Bay) and his pilot, Francois Visscher, went ashore. He explored the country briefly but saw no natives, although he heard some. Next day, 3 December, the surf was too rough for another landing, so a carpenter swam ashore planted a flag, and Tasman took possession of the country, which

he named Van Diemen's Land, and claimed it for Holland.

Continuing east Tasman reached New Zealand. Here three of the *Zeehaen*'s crew were killed by Maoris. Tasman named the spot Murderers' Bay (now Golden Bay) and sailed on. Crossing the entrance to the present Cook Strait, which he took to be a wide, deep bight, Tasman coasted north to the extreme tip of New Zealand, which he called Cape Maria van Diemen, after his employer's wife. In January 1643 some of the islands of the Tongan group were discovered. Further north Tasman searched without success for Mendaña's Solomon Islands, and returned home around the north of New Guinea. Geographically the voyage had been most successful, but as it had tapped no new sources of trade the Dutch felt the money spent on it had been wasted.

Nevertheless, van Diemen sent Tasman off again in 1644 to seek a passage between New Guinea and Australia. As no journal of the voyage survives little is known of it. Like previous Dutch captains Tasman failed to find Torres Strait, but to make up for this he examined and charted about

Governor van Diemen's support for exploration and the persistence of Tasman (left) added much to geographical knowledge. In 1642–3 Tasman discovered Van Diemen's Land, New Zealand, the Tongan Islands and returned to Batavia, having circumnavigated Australia.

2,000 miles of the north coast of New Holland from the Gulf of Carpentaria to de Witt's Land, filling in many gaps. He thus added greatly to geographical knowledge and disproved the theory that the continent was bisected by an inland sea. It was not his fault, nor van Diemen's, that most of what he found was uninviting and barren. Because his achievement brought no dividends to the company, the authorities were again displeased.

In the next fifty years many Dutch ships sighted the west

Torres St.

Duyfken Pt.
R. Wenlock
Cape Keerweer

Gulf of
Carpen-
taria

Arnhem
Land

New Holland

Tropic of
Capricorn

Exmouth Gulf
Pt. Cloates
DeWitts Land
Dirk
Hartogs Is.
Eendracht Land
Houtman
Abrolhos
Edels Land
Nuyts Land
Swan R.
Leeuwin
Land
Rottnest Is.
Great
Australian
Bight
Cape Leeuwin
Nuyts
Archipelago

Dutch discoveries

Van Diemen's
Land

Above : Dutch dis-
coveries in Australia.
The eastern coast was
claimed by the English
in 1770.
Left : the black swan
of Western Australia
first found by
Vlamingh.

14

Vlamingh and his ships reached
Rottnest Island, opposite the
mouth of the Swan River, site
of the present port of Fremantle.

coast, and inevitably there were a number of wrecks. In 1696
Willem de Vlamingh was sent from Amsterdam in the *Geelvink*,
with two smaller ships, to search for one of these. He was
unable to find it, but instead he discovered a fine river
passing through fertile country, which he spent several days
exploring. Because of the numerous black swans, some of
which were captured and taken live to Batavia, Vlamingh
called it the Swan River, and during his survey he passed well
beyond the site of the present city of Perth. Despite Vlamingh's
good report nothing was done to follow up his discovery, and
for a long while New Holland remained an unwanted land.

The English

The first English contact with New Holland was disastrous.
In 1622 the *Tryal*, an East Indiaman, was wrecked on a reef
north of the Monte Bello Islands; and although her captain,
John Brooke, and forty-five others reached Batavia after an
arduous voyage in open boats, eighty-two lives and a valuable
cargo were lost. Another English ship, the *London*, reached
the coast near Houtman's Abrolhos in 1681, but did not linger
in such an inhospitable area.

The first Englishmen actually to go ashore on New Holland
were some buccaneers in the *Cygnet*, which had sailed south
from Timor to escape the vengeful Dutch. Among them was
an adventurer named William Dampier. In January 1688 the
Cygnet was careened for repairs in a bay on the north-west
coast near what is now King Sound, and here Dampier met
some of the local Aborigines, whom he described as 'the
miserablest people in the world'. Back in England Dampier
won fame as the author of *A New Voyage Round the World* and

his piratical exploits were tactfully overlooked. In 1699 he returned to New Holland as commander of HMS *Roebuck*, planning to examine its still-unknown east coast. But he was a poor commander and an unpersevering explorer, and his ship was old and rotten. He landed first at Shark Bay, in search of water, then he sailed north and anchored for awhile among some islands now called the Dampier Archipelago and near the present Roebuck Bay. The area was already well-known to the Dutch, and he made no new discoveries; and as his men were mutinous and his ship leaking badly he left the mainland and sailed for Timor. He cruised for awhile north of New Guinea, and established that this island and New Britain were separated by a strait. But the state of his ship made any thought of examining the east coast of New Holland out of the question; and in fact she sank while at anchor off Ascension Island on the way home, and Dampier and his crew had to beg passages to England in passing ships. Dampier had achieved practically nothing, but he was a colourful character and the accounts of his voyages did much to focus British attention on the South Seas.

In the 1760s three British captains were in the Pacific –

Left: the English buccaneer William Dampier's first meeting with Aborigines.
Below: Dampier and an unusual memorial to him.

WILLIAM DAMPIER
1652   1715

17

Captain James Cook, the great navigator and explorer.

Byron, Wallis and Carteret – but only Carteret, in the *Swallow*, sailed anywhere near Australia when he rediscovered the Solomons in 1767. Two years later the Frenchman Louis Antoine de Bougainville came much closer. After staying awhile in Tahiti he sailed west, rediscovered de Quirós's Espiritu Santo and continued on, hoping to reach the east coast of New Holland. However, off what is now northern Queensland he got so entangled among dangerous coral reefs that he gave up the attempt.

Meanwhile, a converted collier renamed the *Endeavour* had sailed from Plymouth on what was to be one of the great voyages of history. She was commanded by Lieutenant James Cook, the son of a farm-labourer, who had risen from the ranks by sheer ability, and aboard her were Joseph Banks, a wealthy young naturalist, and a staff of scientific observers.

The *Endeavour*'s immediate destination was Tahiti, where the transit of the planet Venus across the face of the sun was to be observed. But Cook also had secret orders to search in high latitudes for the supposed southern continent, and if he failed to find this he was to sail west until he reached New Zealand, and then to return home by whatever route he thought best.

Tahiti was reached in April 1769, and after three months there Cook spent some time exploring and charting several nearby islands which he called the Society Group. Then the *Endeavour* plunged southward, but instead of land all Cook could find was a vast expanse of sea lashed by westerly gales. He reached New Zealand in October and in five months, during which he sailed right round it, he disproved the theory that it was part of the elusive continent and that it was in fact two large islands divided by the narrow strait which Tasman had mistaken for a bight. Rightly this strait now bears Cook's name.

A double Maori war-canoe and a decorated club.

Having charted New Zealand with remarkable accuracy Cook consulted his officers as to the best route home. As winter was approaching a plan to sail east by way of Cape Horn was rejected, and instead Cook decided to explore the still-unknown east coast of New Holland.

At daybreak on 20 April 1770 Cook's first lieutenant, Zachary Hicks, reported land ahead. Cook called the spot Point Hicks, but it is now known as Cape Everard, on the east coast of Victoria. The land was undulating and well-wooded and seemed fertile, and the smoke from many fires suggested it was well inhabited. For some days the *Endeavour* coasted northward looking for a good anchorage, but the only one in the area, Twofold Bay, was missed in the night. On a beach near Red Point some Aborigines were seen, and Cook and Banks tried to go ashore in a yawl. However, the natives fled and the surf was too heavy to risk a landing. Next morning the

Left: fishing methods of east-coast Aborigines.
Right: Cook's landing at Botany Bay, opposed by Aborigines.

ship was outside a large and sheltered bay. Cook decided to go in, and by 2 p.m. she was at anchor off the south shore. As Cook and some of his people attempted to land they were opposed by two natives who threw stones and spears, until they were peppered with small shot and sent running for cover. In the next few days while Cook and others explored the bay they often saw natives, but all attempts to win their friendship failed. Cook was very impressed, particularly with the land at the head of the bay which, he wrote, was 'as fine meadow as ever was seen'. Some large stingrays were caught and for a while Cook thought of calling the place Stingrays Harbour. But because of the great number of unique plants collected by Banks and his people he changed his mind and named it Botany Bay. The English colours were displayed every day, and the ship's name and date were cut into a tree. The tree has now disappeared, but at Kurnell an obelisk marks the spot where Cook first landed.

After a little more than a week the *Endeavour* resumed her way north. Nine miles beyond Botany Bay she passed the entrance to another harbour which Cook named Port Jackson after an official of the Admiralty. By not going in he missed discovering one of the safest harbours in the world, on which the city of Sydney was to rise. A little further north he missed

Above: Cook claims possession of New South Wales.
Right: the *Endeavour* careened for repairs after running on a reef.

another prize when he sailed past 'a small round rock'. This is now Nobby's Head, and on the banks of the Hunter River beyond it stands the industrial city of Newcastle. On 16 May the *Endeavour* passed Point Danger, which marks the border between the present States of New South Wales and Queensland; and next day she passed a wide, open bay the waters of which were so pale that Cook assumed a large river must run into it. He was right, and on its banks now stands Brisbane, the capital of Queensland.

Soon afterwards Cook noted that the sea was surprisingly calm, but was unaware that he was now sailing within the protective wall of the Great Barrier Reef. The discovery came soon enough, however, for on the night of 11th June the *Endeavour* ran aground on a coral reef and stuck fast. For almost twenty-four hours she was in danger of becoming a total wreck, but guns, ballast and other heavy articles were

jettisoned to lighten her, and eventually Cook was able to have her hauled clear. Three days later he sailed her into a small stream which he called the Endeavour River, and she was careened. While the carpenters were repairing her and later while Cook awaited a favourable wind to resume the voyage, contact of a sort was made with the local Aborigines. Banks found many exotic plants, and a strange animal was shot which hopped on powerful hind legs and which the natives called a kangaroo.

On his way again Cook found himself among such a maze of reefs that he avoided them for awhile by standing out to the open sea. Late in August he finally proved that Australia and New Guinea were separated by sailing through and naming Endeavour Strait; and he landed on a small island and took possession for England of the whole coastline he had discovered. He named it New South Wales.

First settlement

For more than a century Britain had sent many of her convicted criminals to the American colonies, but the loss of these in the War of Independence meant that she could no longer do so. As a result jails and old ships turned into prison hulks were soon overcrowded, and it became obvious that some other dumping ground must be found. Joseph Banks and James Matra, a former midshipman on the *Endeavour*, had already suggested Botany Bay as a site for a penal colony, and in 1786 the government decided to act on their advice.

With Captain Arthur Phillip, an extremely able but little-known naval officer in charge, what we now know as the First Fleet sailed from England on 13 May 1787. It comprised HMS's *Sirius* and *Supply*, six convict transports and three storeships, which carried supplies for two years. On board,

Converted hulks eased prison overcrowding in England.

in addition to the crews, were 568 male and 191 female convicts with 13 children, 206 marines with 46 wives and children, and 20 officials – a total of 1044, who were to be the founders of the new colony.

Phillip was to be governor, and Captain John Hunter of the *Sirius* had authority to take over in the event of Phillip's death. Major Robert Ross, commanding the marines, was lieutenant-governor, Captain David Collins was in charge of legal affairs as judge-advocate, John White was surgeon-general and the Reverend Richard Johnson was chaplain.

The voyage was comparatively uneventful, and by 20 January 1788 all eleven ships were safely in Botany Bay. Only twenty-three convicts had died, and most of these had been ill before they set out.

Phillip realized at once that Botany Bay was unsuitable.

Governor Arthur Phillip and the First Fleet at Botany Bay.

Next day he and some others rowed north to Port Jackson, and were delighted by its capaciousness and safety. As a site for the settlement Phillip chose a cove a few miles up the harbour which had good anchorage. He called it Sydney Cove, after the Secretary of State for the Colonies.

The British flag was hoisted on 26 January, which is now celebrated as Australia Day, and next morning work began on felling trees, clearing ground, unloading stores and erecting tents. Two weeks later all the colonists, bond and free, assembled to hear Phillip's commission read; and three days after that, with Lieutenant Philip Gidley King in charge, the *Supply* sailed with convicts and marines to form a subsidiary settlement at Norfolk Island.

The governor faced many problems. Few convicts were willing to work harder than they had to. Some strayed into the woods and were attacked by Aborigines. The stealing of food from the government stores was prevalent, and there was much drunkenness and immorality. Major Ross was uncooperative and would not allow his marines to act as convict overseers. Some of the small stock of sheep died, and cattle strayed and could not be found. Crops were planted in what are now the Botanical Gardens – hence the name Farm Cove – but mice and ants ate the grain before it germinated.

Left : Sydney Cove, Aug. 1788.
Above : the governor's native friend Benelong.
Below : toasting success to the new colony.

In general the soil around Sydney was poor. However, at the head of the harbour, about fourteen miles away, Phillip found ample good land and formed a second settlement there, which he called Rose Hill but which soon became better-known by its native name of Parramatta.

By the middle of 1789 little food remained, and rations had

Port Jackson and Sydney Cove.
Brickfield Hill on the high road to Parramatta.

to be reduced. The *Sirius* was sent to Cape Town for supplies but returned with only a small supply of flour. As Norfolk Island had proved extremely fertile Phillip decided to send about a third of his people there to ease the situation. The result was disastrous. The *Sirius* was wrecked and those aboard were marooned on the island for almost a year. By

Government House, Sydney.
A view of Government Farm at Rose Hill

Wreck of the *Sirius* at Norfolk Island.

early 1790 few convicts at Sydney and Parramatta had the strength to work, and some died as they toiled in the fields.

The arrival of more convict transports and a storeship from England averted actual famine, but faced Phillip with other problems. Convicts aboard this second fleet, as it became known, had been treated so inhumanely that a quarter of them had died on the voyage out. Others died soon after landing, and few were capable of work. Conditions aboard the ships of the third fleet, which arrived during July and August 1791, were not bad. Even so, there were many deaths.

Although himself in poor health Phillip led several expeditions north and west of Sydney in search of better land. On one of these the Hawkesbury River was discovered, and within a few years townships had been formed and thousands of acres of its rich alluvial flats were under crop. Phillip's health declined further when he was speared by an Aborigine at Manly, but in December 1792 he returned to England, still

Governor Phillip wounded by a native at Manly Cove.

confident, in spite of everything, that the colony he had founded would one day become Britain's proudest possession.

By this time the marines had been relieved by the New South Wales Corps, especially recruited for garrison duty in the colony, and for almost three years the place was run by its commanding officer, Major Francis Grose. Grose greatly favoured his officers. He made them magistrates, gave them land and free convict labour, and allowed them to establish themselves as merchants. Thus encouraged they soon created a trading monopoly and enriched themselves by importing rum and using it instead of money to buy and sell and to pay wages. Among those who benefited in this way was Lieutenant John Macarthur, a man of few scruples but great vision, who soon became convinced that the colony's future prosperity lay in fine-wool sheep.

The Platypus

Bass and Flinders ride out a storm in *Tom Thumb*.

When Captain Hunter returned to the colony in 1795 as second governor he did his best to break the power of the officers, but he was a gentle man with no gift for intrigue and his opponents were more than a match for him. They did much to blacken his name in influential circles in London, and as a result of this campaign he was recalled in 1800. The letter was carried by Philip Gidley King, now a post captain, and on Whitehall's instruction it was to King as third governor that Hunter handed over when he left in September 1800.

Hunter had been accompanied to the colony by two friends from Lincolnshire – George Bass, ship's surgeon, and Matthew Flinders, a young lieutenant. Both were eager to explore the coast of New South Wales, which was still almost unknown, and with this in view Bass had brought a small dinghy which he called 'Tom Thumb'. In this, with a boy as crew, they sailed south from Sydney about fifty miles and landed near what is now Port Kembla to dry out their stores and gunpowder. Hostile natives appeared, but Flinders soon won them over by producing scissors and trimming their hair and beards.

In 1797 Bass set out, more ambitiously, in a whaleboat and explored the whole coast as far south as a harbour he called Westernport. Here an ocean swell from the south-west convinced him that contrary to the general belief Van Diemen's Land, which lay further south, was an island. If this were true it would reduce sailing time from England by up to a fortnight, and Governor Hunter sent Bass and Flinders in the *Norfolk*, a twenty-five-ton sloop, to investigate. They proved the point by sailing right round Van Diemen's Land, charting as they went, and the strait they discovered was fittingly named Bass Strait. A little later Flinders spent six weeks in the *Norfolk* examining the coast as far north from Sydney as Hervey Bay, in what is now Queensland. His taste for exploration had now become a passion, and by the time he returned to England he had conceived the idea of examining and charting the coastline of New Holland.

Flinders turns barber to win over hostile natives.

Flinders

Early in 1801 some alarm was caused in England by the news that two French ships, the *Géographe* and *Naturaliste,* had set out for New Holland on what was officially a scientific expedition. The expedition was regarded with some suspicion because Napoleon's colonial ambitions were well known and much of New Holland was still open to anyone who cared to claim it. Flinders having returned to London easily persuaded the Admiralty to send him back to New Holland to carry out his ambitious charting project and so frustrate any French plans to claim part of the continent. While his ship, the *Investigator,* was fitting out Flinders married a childhood sweetheart, but permission for her to sail with him was firmly refused when she was found aboard, 'not even wearing a bonnet', as one scandalized official reported.

The French ships already had a start of nine months when Flinders sailed in July 1801. New Holland was reached near

Seals, kangaroos and emus lived amicably on Kangaroo Island.

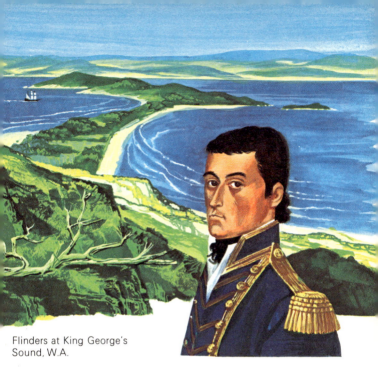

Flinders at King George's Sound, W.A.

Cape Leeuwin in December, and the *Investigator* spent some weeks in King George's Sound, where Albany now stands. From here Flinders coasted slowly east, charting meticulously as he went. It was dangerous work and several times only his skill averted disaster. It came at last, however, when a cutter sent to seek fresh water was caught in a riptide and her crew of eight were drowned. About here the coastline turned abruptly north, and Flinders hoped it might lead to an inland sea. Instead he found himself in a deep gulf which he named after Lord Spencer of the Admiralty. Soon afterwards he discovered a large island on which kangaroos, seals and emus lived, as he wrote, 'in perfect amity'. He called it Kangaroo Island. Back on the mainland he found and named St Vincent's Gulf, and sailed close to the site of the present city of Adelaide.

Flinders still had no idea where the French ships were, but he was soon to find out. On 8 April a strange sail was recog-

Spencer Gulf

Encounter Bay

Sydney

Kangaroo Is.

Port Phillip

Cape Leeuwin

King's George's Sound

King Is.

Flinder s track

nized as the *Géographe*, and, taking no chances, Flinders had the *Investigator's* decks cleared for action. However, the intentions of the French commander, Nicholas Baudin, were peaceful. Both ships hove to, and through an interpreter Flinders and Baudin had a long conference. Flinders was delighted to learn that the French had spent some months in Van Diemen's Land, 'picking up shells and catching butter-flies', as one officer remarked disgustedly, and had only cursorily explored about 500 miles of the mainland shore of Bass Strait. The *Géographe* and the *Naturaliste* had lost contact in a gale, and Baudin assumed correctly that the *Naturaliste* had sailed on to Sydney. It was obvious that Baudin would need to do the same soon for his own ship needed repair, and many of his crew were down with scurvy. Next day Baudin continued west and Flinders east. Although Baudin was now doubling on Flinders's tracks he charted and renamed geo-graphical features as he went, and on his map he called the area Terre Napoleon. On his way to Sydney, Flinders found a large harbour which Baudin had missed. He thought he had made a major discovery, and was chagrined later to learn that Lieutenant John Murray, in the *Lady Nelson*, had beaten him to it by a mere ten weeks. Hunter's successor as governor, Captain P. G. King, called it Port Phillip after the founder of the colony, and on its shores now stand the cities of Melbourne and Geelong.

The *Investigator*, herself badly in need of repair, reached Sydney on 9 May. Flinders found that conditions there had changed little for the better. Governor King had had no more success than Hunter in curbing the power of the military monopolists, and the evil effects of rum as currecy were seriously retarding progress. Eventually as King had hoped, the corrupt officers quarrelled among themselves and Macarthur had been sent to England to be court-martialled for wounding Colonel William Paterson in a duel.

The *Naturaliste* was already in port, and in June the *Géographe* arrived, her crew so scurvy-ridden that Flinders had to send men to help sail her in. King did all he could for the sick, but some of Baudin's officers repaid this kindness by collecting information about Sydney's garrison strength and examining beaches in which invasion troops might land.

On 22 July the patched-up *Investigator* was on her way again, accompanied by the *Lady Nelson*, a vessel of 60 tons with sliding keels. Although useful in shallow water the *Lady Nelson* was so slow that Flinders sent her back to Sydney. Three months were spent on a painstaking survey of the present Queensland coast, and Flinders filled in many gaps left by Cook. By November the *Investigator* was in the Gulf of Carpentaria, leaking so badly that Flinders had to beach her. Her timbers were so rotten that it was doubtful whether she

Captain Nicholas Baudin and the *Géographe*.

Above : Flinders finds Aboriginal cave paintings on Groote Eylandt.
Right : Malayan fishing proas off the north coast.
Below : Aboriginal bark painting of a proa by a native artist of
Groote Eylandt. Subjects of this kind were not commonly chosen.

would survive a storm, and prudence demanded that the expedition should return to Sydney.

But Flinders was now a man obsessed, and despite the heat and constant rain, despite the many dangers which included attacks by Aborigines, he continued his survey. Four months later, with provisions low and his ship barely holding together, he was forced to give up and head for the Dutch port of Koepang in Timor, where his crumbling ship was patched up. The weather made a return to Sydney through Torres Strait impracticable, and Flinders had to sail the long route around the west and south coasts of the continent. The voyage took two months, and it was a nightmare for all. Four men died from dysentery, Flinders could hardly move for scorbutic sores, and few of his crew were fit for duty. Sydney was reached on 9 June 1803, and within a few days four more men were dead.

Although still not fully recovered Flinders was impatient to get to England to report what he had achieved and to obtain another ship for his survey, replacing the *Investigator*, which had now been condemned. He divided his company

Wreck of the *Porpoise* and *Cato.*

between HMS *Porpoise*, which King had lent him, and a merchant ship, the *Cato,* which was on her way to China. When they left Sydney on 10 August they were accompanied by another merchantman, the *Bridgewater*. At night a week later the *Porpoise* and *Cato* were wrecked on a coral reef about 250 miles off the Queensland coast, and the *Bridgewater,* after hovering about for awhile, sailed on and left them to their fate. Fortunately only three men were drowned, and before the ships broke up the survivors and almost all the stores were landed on a sandbank about 300 yards long. In a six-oared cutter with a volunteer crew Flinders returned to Sydney, about 750 miles south; and those remaining on the sandbank were rescued after almost two months.

Some returned to Sydney and some went on to China. But Flinders, as impatient as ever, made for England in a barely seaworthy schooner of 29 tons called the *Cumberland*. In the mistaken belief that England and France were still at peace he put in to Mauritius for repairs and reprovisioning. He was received with some suspicion, and made the tactical mistake of refusing to dine with the governor, General Decaen. As a result his schooner was seized and he and his crew were arrested. It took Sir Joseph Banks and others six years to obtain his release, and when Flinders returned to England in 1810 he was broken in health. The last remnants of his failing energy were thrown into writing *A Voyage to Terra Australis*, which with its superb charts is now one of the classic accounts of exploration by sea. Flinders never saw the book. When the first copy was delivered by the publishers he was unconscious, and he died next day, 19 July 1814 – a gaunt, grey-haired old man of forty.

A rescue ship finds survivors on Wreck Reef.

Van Diemen's Land

Meanwhile, in spite of internal dissension, the colony was steadily expanding. About seventy miles north of Sydney a splendid river had been found in 1797 and named for Governor Hunter, but because of rich deposits of coal in the area it became better-known as the Coal River. A settlement founded there in 1801 and called Newcastle was abandoned soon afterwards, but on orders from England it was re-established in 1804 as a penal station for convicts who had committed further crimes in the colony. As such it soon developed a grim reputation. West of Sydney there were now many farms between Parramatta and the Hawkesbury, and on the Hawkesbury itself were several small but thriving townships. To the south-west herds of wild cattle, descended from the strays of 1788, had been found grazing on rich land which became known as the Cowpastures; and here John Macarthur, who had resigned his commission and returned as a private citizen, established himself as a breeder of Merino sheep on a 5,000 acres grant made to him by Earl Camden. Nevertheless, the settled area still remained hardly more than a pinpoint on the map of the continent. As yet nobody knew what lay in the vast area west of the Blue Mountains, for despite many attempts nobody had succeeded in crossing them.

Left: Green Hills on the Hawkesbury.
Above: Macarthur and his flock.
Below: Macarthur's home.

The visit to Sydney of Baudin's ships had increased Governor King's fears of French intentions in New Holland. When he heard of boastful reports by some of the French officers he wrote to England urging that a new settlement be formed at Port Phillip, and sent Lieutenant Charles Robbins to find the French ships, which were still somewhere in Bass Strait. Robbins located them at King Island, handed Baudin a letter of warning from the governor, and nailed the British colours to a tree. Baudin thought the gesture childish and

Above: Col. David Collins.
Below: St Phillip's, Sydney.

wrote a mild protest to King, and soon afterwards his ships sailed for Mauritius. Even so King remained suspicious, and in August 1803 he sent Lieutenant John Bowen with some troops and convicts to found a small settlement on the River Derwent in Van Diemen's Land.

In the meantime an earlier letter sent by King to England had drawn an unusually quick response, and within weeks an expedition was being formed to occupy Port Phillip. The colony's first judge-advocate, David Collins, now a colonel, was appointed to command it; HMS *Calcutta* which was taking aboard 300 convicts for Sydney, was diverted to the new destination; and the *Ocean* was chartered to convey settlers and stores.

When the ships left on 27 April 1803 they carried about 470 colonists, comprising convicts, civil officers, marines, free settlers, wives

and children. In a storm the ships were separated, and the *Ocean* reached Port Phillip two days before the *Calcutta*. Water was found by sinking casks in sandy soil at a bay to the east of the entrance, near the present town of Sorrento, and while people and stores were being landed Collins sent a party to look for a more suitable site. They missed the River Yarra, on which Melbourne was to rise, and though they found good land on the western shore, near present-day Geelong, the natives there were numerous and fierce. Disappointed, Collins wrote asking King's permission to move elsewhere. The poor discipline of his marines and the frequent escapes of convicts into the bush added to his worries, and he was relieved when King authorised him to move either to the Derwent or to Port Dalrymple on the north coast of Van Diemen's Land. He chose the former and the move was made early in 1804. Soon afterwards, to ensure command of Bass Strait, King sent Colonel Paterson with troops and convicts to occupy Port Dalrymple. With two settlements on the island he felt he had no further need to worry about French colonial ambitions there.

Lieutenant Robbins shows the flag.

The first settlement at Port Phillip.

Risdon Cove, on the Derwent River, where Bowen had settled his people, was rejected by Collins in favour of a better site a few miles downstream, and here rose the tents and huts which were one day to become the city of Hobart. For awhile all went well, the convicts worked hard and few gave trouble. The free settlers were industrious, the natives were friendly, and although food stocks were dwindling Collins confidently expected more from England. However, the position soon deteriorated. Convict absconders, who became known as bushrangers, plundered the settlers and maltreated the natives. As no food-ship had arrived from England, Collins sent out hunters to bring in kangaroo meat, which was plentiful. The natives, driven from their hunting grounds, turned hostile and it became dangerous to venture unarmed into the bush. Governor King sent some salt meat from Sydney but most of it was uneatable, and by the end of 1805 the settlement was facing famine. The chaplain, Reverend Robert Knopwood, wrote that the weekly ration sufficed only for a day and a half; and Lieutenant Edward Lord said that he was often glad 'to go to bed for want of bread'.

With increased local harvests, a cargo of rice from India and some help from Sydney the food crisis was over in another year. But it was soon replaced by another: the British government had decided to abandon Norfolk Island, and about 550 settlers were removed to the Derwent, more than doubling its population, all demanding promised compensation and convict labour which Collins was unable to supply.

In August 1806, William Bligh (of the famous mutiny of the *Bounty* seventeen years before) had been sent out to replace King as governor. He had been instructed by Whitehall to break the monopolistic power of the officers and to abolish the traffic in rum, and to achieve these ends had introduced drastic regulations. Led by Macarthur the officers fought to retain their privileges, and a climax was reached when Macarthur defied the governor's authority and was arrested for sedition. A court-martial, composed of his friends, refused to try him; and the same evening (26 January 1808) Major George Johnston, the senior officer then in Sydney, marched on Government House. At the entrance his troops were defied by Bligh's daughter, Mary Putland, and had to push her aside before they could find and arrest the governor.

Hobart Town in the early days.

Collins was shocked to learn what had happened, and smuggled a letter to Bligh assuring him of his loyalty. During a year under arrest Bligh made himself so obnoxious that the rebels were ready to get rid of him on any terms, and gave him command of HMS *Porpoise* on condition that he sailed directly to England. Instead he went to Derwent, relying on Collins's support and to await the arrival of a new governor. Though friendly at first, relations between Bligh and Collins soon became strained. Norfolk Island settlers who remained stubbornly loyal to Bligh were punished, and Bligh retaliated by flogging Collins's natural son George, who was a midshipman on the *Porpoise*. Banned from going ashore, Bligh sailed down to the Derwent estuary, intercepted passing ships, helped himself to stores from government vessels, and bought food destined for the settlement from merchant ships. This absurd and intolerable situation lasted almost six months. Then in January 1810 Bligh learned that a new governor was on his way to Sydney, and the *Porpoise* sailed for Port Jackson. Collins made no attempt to hide his relief. To his brother in England he wrote that although he still believed Bligh had been illegally deposed he felt that his tyrannical behaviour had warranted more than mere suspension, 'unless from the end of a strong halter'.

Far left: Bligh's
daughter, Mary
Putland, defies the
rebels outside
Government House.
Above: a derogatory
cartoon which rep-
resents Governor
Bligh being found
under a bed and
about to be put under
arrest.
Left: Captain William
Bligh, deposed as
governor by the
militant N.S.W. Corps.

The way to the west

The new governor, Colonel Lachlan Macquarie, had one great advantage over his predecessors: he had brought to the colony his own regiment, the 73rd, and his first act was to disband the N.S.W. Corps. All regulations and land grants issued by the rebel government were annulled, Bligh's supporters who had been imprisoned were released, and Johnston was arrested and sent to England for court-martial.

While Bligh was still in Sydney assembling evidence for the prosecution word was received of the sudden death of Collins from heart-failure. Bligh has often been blamed for having driven him to the grave, but more likely his death was due to an accumulation of worries over the years caused by the complete and unpardonable neglect of the Derwent settlement by the authorities in London. Lord, as senior officer at Hobart Town, gave Collins a state funeral and presented a

Governor Lachlan Macquarie and his wife Elizabeth.

bill for £700. Macquarie was horrified, but did not oppose its payment.

In New South Wales there were many urgent problems. Floods on the Hawkesbury had destroyed several harvests, and now a long drought was withering crops and pastures. If the colony was to progress, if grazing land was to be found for its growing flocks and herds, expansion was essential, particularly westward.

But the way to the west was still barred by the seemingly impassable barrier of the Blue Mountains. Earlier explorers had tried to force a path through the rugged and eroded valleys of the range. In 1813 new tactics were tried by a party led by Gregory Blaxland, a settler, William Charles Wentworth, son of the colonial surgeon, and William Lawson, a retired army officer. By keeping to the crests of the ridges they managed to reach a point they called Mount Blaxland after seventeen

A wife-auction at Windsor earned punishment for all.

arduous days, and though they did not complete the crossing they proved it possible. To the west they saw a vast tract of good, well-watered land, sufficient, they told Macquarie, to serve the colony's needs for thirty years. Soon afterwards George William Evans, a government surveyor, followed their tracks and pushed on another hundred miles, mostly along the banks of a river he called the Macquarie.

Evans's report of the country he had traversed was so

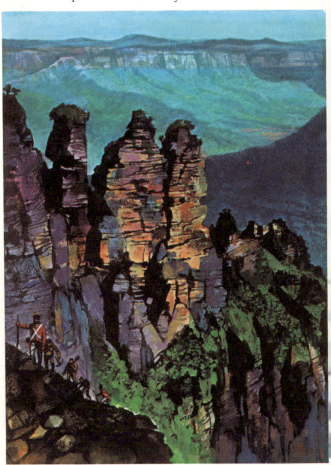

Left: the Three Sisters, Blue Mountains, with Jamieson Valley in
the background.
Above: whaling off the Australian coast

favourable that Macquarie decided to have a road built over
the mountains. The task was entrusted to William Cox, a
prosperous settler. Cox chose a gang of thirty convicts who
were promised their freedom if they worked well. They
worked so well indeed that in six months they completed
more than a hundred miles of road through rugged mountain
country and built a dozen bridges. Cox's own reward for this
remarkable feat was a grant of 2,000 acres, the first west of the
mountains.

In 1815 Macquarie and his wife led a vice-regal progress
of about fifty people over the new road, and in nine days
reached a point on the Macquarie River where the governor
decreed that a town should be laid out and named after Earl
Bathurst, the then Secretary of State for the Colonies. Land-
hungry settlers followed close behind with laden bullock
wagons and their flocks, often with their wives and families.
Some were given land, others simply stopped where they
chose. Australia's great squatting era had begun.

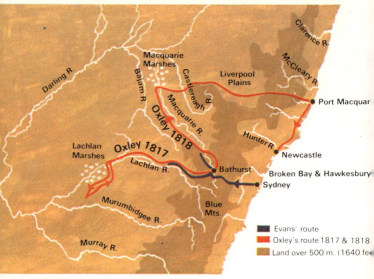

Exploration routes of Evans and Oxley.

Instead of returning to Sydney with the governor Evans now led a small party to explore the country south-west of Bathurst. In ten days he found another river which he called the Lachlan, after Macquarie's son. He described the country in its vicinity as 'a second Hawkesbury'; and in an enthusiastic report to London Macquarie wrote that it possessed 'many and important advantages for a numerous population'.

It seems likely that the colony's surveyor-general, John Oxley, was jealous of his subordinate's success, for a ruling came from London that future similar expeditions should be led by 'some person of more scientific observation', who could record details of country, soil, animals, vegetation, minerals and the customs and language of the Aborigines. The nearest available approach to such a paragon was Oxley himself; and in 1817 when Macquarie sent another expedition to try to solve the problem of the western rivers it was led by Oxley with Evans as his second in command. Having reached the Lachlan, Oxley followed it downstream for some distance. Then it suddenly disappeared into extensive and apparently impenetrable swamps, and after a futile week Oxley decided to quit it and strike south-west. His route led through thick, parched, waterless scrub, and his horses were soon in poor shape. Had Oxley persisted he would have found the Murrumbidgee River, but instead he turned north, got involved again in the Lachlan swamps and finally gave up, convinced that the interior west of a certain meridian was so devoid of wood, water and grass as to be uninhabitable.

In June 1818 Oxley set out once more, again with Evans as his second. This time he tried to follow the Macquarie downstream, only to find that, like the Lachlan, it also lost itself in a huge swamp. While Oxley tried vainly to get through this, Evans led a small party east, and in a few days found a river running roughly parallel with the Macquarie which was called the Castlereagh. Abandoning the Macquarie swamps Oxley crossed to the Castlereagh and continued on to the Warrumbungle Ranges, from the summits of which he hoped to get a clear picture of the layout of the interior. The view westward yielded little, but further east he saw a great tract of rich grazing land which he named the Liverpool Plains. Crossing

Oxley on the track.

Early prize fighting.

Natives attack an early settler's hut.

these the party climbed arduously over the main Dividing Range, made a hazardous descent and followed a river to the sea. Oxley called it the Hastings and the harbour into which it flowed Port Macquarie. From there the explorers made an arduous jouney down the coast to Newcastle.

As always, squatters followed close behind, though the Liverpool Plains themselves were to remain inaccessible for another five years. Life was not easy for these pioneers. They had no legal title to the land they occupied. They were far from civilization, and had only rough bush tracks over which to haul their possessions and stores and to convey their wool to market. They built and lived in rough slab huts, devoid of almost all comforts. Their diet was adequate but monotonous. Their sheep strayed or were harassed by dingoes or killed by Aborigines. Their intrusion into the native hunting grounds was bitterly resented, and they were often attacked and not infrequently killed. Yet the stream westward continued, and Macquarie, realizing that it was impossible to restrain it, did not try.

In Sydney the governor was having troubles of his own. He believed that when a convict had expiated his crime he was entitled to the privileges of a free man, and some of his best friends were emancipists. This policy was opposed by prosperous free settlers and merchant who became known as 'exclusives' and complained to their powerful friends in London. There was also much official criticism of Macquarie's passion for building, not because the colony did not need churches, hospitals, bridges, barracks and jails but because of their cost. Eventually a commissioner, J. T. Bigge, was sent to inquire into all aspects of Macquarie's administration. His reports were not favourable, and in 1821 while Macquarie was touring Van Diemen's Land he received word of his recall. He left for England soon afterwards. In a vigorous defence of his twelve years' rule Macquarie pointed out that in that time the colony's population had risen from 12,000 to 38,000, its acres under crop had quadrupled, its livestock had increased tenfold, its revenue had soared and its moral climate had improved infinitely in every way.

Convicts at hard labour on the treadmill.

Some of Governor Macquarie's buildings.
Above: the female factory at Parramatta.
Below: St. James' Church.
Above right: St Matthew's, Windsor.
Right: the centre block of Sydney Hospital.
Below right: the lighthouse at South Head.

Lifting the veil

Macquarie's successor, General Sir Thomas Brisbane, has been criticized for giving more of his time to astronomy than to the colony he had been sent to govern. Nevertheless, there was much progress and expansion during his four years there.

In 1823 Captain Mark Currie, R.N., with Brigade-Major John Ovens and a skilled bushman, Jonathan Wild, made a short excursion south from Lake George, near what is now Canberra, and found a large area of rich land beyond the Murrumbidgee River. They called this Brisbane Downs, but it soon became and remains known by its native name, Monaro. About the same time Allan Cunningham, a botanist, set out with four companions to find a route through the rugged mountains that barred access from Bathurst to the Liverpool Plains. Despite several failures and shortage of food Cunningham persisted, and after 'a very laborious and harassing journey' discovered what he called Pandora's Pass. Squatters followed close behind, and by the year's end stock were grazing on the newly-opened plains.

In the same year the surveyor-general, John Oxley, was sent north in the cutter *Mermaid* to report on Port Curtis and

Memorial to the explorer Oxley at Brisbane.

Brisbane penal station (above) and convict conditions.

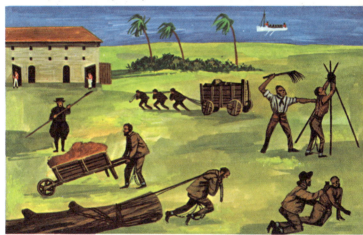

Moreton Bay as possible sites for a penal settlement. Port Curtis was quickly rejected and Oxley concentrated on Moreton Bay. Here he found two shipwrecked convicts who had lived for some months with the local natives. They told him of a large river up which he rowed for about fifty miles, and which he named after the governor. In 1824 he returned and established a convict station at Redcliffe, but later this was relocated on the site of the present city of Brisbane. Oxley's health was failing, and when he died in 1828 he was

Above: Hume and Hovell and (right) their track to Port Phillip.

succeeded as Surveyor-General by Major Thomas Livingstone Mitchell, a veteran of the Peninsular war.

Meanwhile Hamilton Hume, a young settler, and William Hovell, a retired sea-captain, had set out in October 1824 from Hume's station near Lake George to reach the south coast. The governor had wanted them to make for Spencer's Gulf, but as he had declined to finance the expedition they chose instead to head for Westernport, on the shore of Bass Strait. Almost from the start they quarrelled about the route they should take. They found the Murrumbidgee in flood and crossed it by turning a cart into a punt with the aid of a tarpaulin. The country beyond was broken and difficult, but well-grassed and good grazing land. From the crest of a ridge they saw before them a majestic range of snow-capped mountains and personal differences were forgotten as they gazed in awe, the first white men to see the Australian Alps. Skirting this formidable barrier they crossed a wide river which Hume named for his father. By now their quarrels had become so constant that at one stage they decided to separate.

Their only frying-pan was broken in a tug-of-war as to who should have it, and they even thought of cutting their tent in two. However, good sense prevailed and they continued on together. In what is now eastern Victoria they crossed the Mitta Mitta, Ovens and Goulburn rivers and eventually reached what they took to be Westernport, but Hovell's calculations were so far out that in fact they were at Corio Bay, Port Phillip, on the site of Gee-long. The error was not discovered for a long time, though years later Hume

Governor
George Arthur.

63

claimed proudly that he had known about this all along.

Cunningham was active again in 1827 when he pushed north from the Liverpool Plains and found the Gwydir, Macintyre and Condamine rivers, all flowing west. Beyond he came on a vast tract of splendid grazing land which he called the Darling Downs after Sir Ralph Darling, who had succeeded Brisbane as governor. These lay inland from Moreton Bay, divided from it by a mountain range, and in 1828 Cunningham tried to find a way through this barrier from the Coast. He failed, however, and when squatters moved in to the downs they followed his original inland track.

The discovery of so many new rivers had revived speculation about the existence of an inland sea, and in December 1828 Captain Charles Sturt with Hume as his second-in-command set out from Wellington, on the Macquarie, in an attempt to settle the point. Like Oxley ten years earlier he failed to get through the Macquarie marshes, but skirted them instead, and eventually reached a large river into which the Macquarie flowed, and which he called the Darling. It was a year of drought and the river had dwindled to a mere chain of salt pools, and after following it down for about sixty miles Sturt was forced to give up.

Above: the Post Office, Sydney. Sturt in the Macquarie Marshes (left), being pursued by natives on the Murray River (right).

Late in the same year, 1829, Sturt was given command of an expedition to trace the course of the Murrumbidgee. Near its junction with the Lachlan he formed a depot, where he left some of his men with stores. A whaleboat which had been carried in sections was assembled, a skiff was built to carry food and equipment, and with seven companions Sturt set off to complete the journey by water. After only two days the skiff struck a submerged log and sank, and although the provisions it had carried were recovered most were spoiled and had to be discarded. A few days later the whaleboat suddenly entered 'a broad and noble stream', which Sturt called the Murray after an English statesman, not aware that it was actually the lower part of the Hume. Natives were numerous, and though Sturt and his party treated them kindly and with great tolerance they were several times in danger of attack. On one occasion some hundreds of natives crowded on to a sandspit, shouting angrily and waving their spears, and as the boat could not avoid coming into range a clash seemed inevitable. At the critical moment, however, a native who had become friendly with Sturt dived into the river, swam to the sandbank, and persuaded the others to put up their weapons. Near where this occurred 'a new and beautiful stream' joined the Murray, and Sturt guessed correctly that it was the Darling, whose upper reaches he had discovered a year earlier. After some days the Murray turned sharply south, and on 9 February 1830 the explorers reached its mouth, a wide, shallow lake separated by sandhills from the sea, which

Australia's first steamship, the *Sophia Jane*.

Sturt and his first two exploration routes.

Sturt called Lake Alexandrina after the future Queen Victoria.

The return journey upstream was a protracted ordeal for all. Sturt and his men were already exhausted, and although an occasional following breeze enabled them to raise sail, most of the time they had to row against the strong current. It became, in fact, a race against starvation as food stocks were now desperately low. Every day they rowed from dawn until dusk, with only an hour's break at noon, and even when men collapsed or fell asleep at the oars they pressed on. From the Murrumbidgee entrance to Lake Alexandrina on the outward journey had taken them twenty-six days; the return, fighting every yard of the way, took them only twenty-three, a remarkable achievement. To their dismay they found the Murrumbidgee in flood and running much more strongly than before. After six days they reached the depot where they had embarked, only to discover it deserted. For another agonizing seventeen days the half-starved men pulled against the current, kept going only by Sturt's heroic example. At last they could go no further. They were still ninety miles from Wantabadgery, the nearest outpost of civilization, and two men set out to walk there. For six uncertain days Sturt and his companions awaited their return, and when they finally appeared with horses and a drayload of food the last ounce of flour had been eaten. The journey back to Sydney was by easy stages. Although all had survived, the long ordeal had left its mark, and for awhile afterwards Sturt was blind.

The expedition had added much to geographical knowledge and Sturt was acclaimed by all but Major Mitchell, who felt it was his own right as surveyor-general to lead all explorations and to reap any resulting honour and glory. This view was not shared by Governor Darling, who had good reason to regard Mitchell as arrogant and over-ambitious and felt that his time would be better spent catching up on departmental arrears.

But Darling was recalled late in 1831, and in the six weeks before his successor, Sir Richard Bourke, arrived Mitchell won the permission of the acting-governor, Colonel Lindesay, to search for a supposed large river called by natives the Kindur,

Port Arthur penal settlement, Van Diemen's Land.

Above: Natives of the Darling River.
Right: Major Mitchell, surveyor-general and explorer.

which was said to flow northward to the Gulf of Carpentaria. The only dubious authority for its existence was a convict escapee who claimed to have found it, but this was enough for Mitchell, who set out in November 1831 with a party of seventeen. In fact there was no such river, and all Mitchell discovered was the Macintyre, a tributary of the Darling. Two men were killed by Aborigines, who also stole most of the provisions, and after two months Mitchell had to return to Sydney, having achieved little.

For awhile there was a lull, and squatters did their own exploring as they pushed out into unknown country with their flocks and herds. Then in 1835 Mitchell set off again, this time hoping to disprove Sturt's theory that the Darling flowed into the Murray. At an early stage Richard Cunningham, a brother of the botanist-explorer, strayed and was murdered by natives. Nevertheless, Mitchell pressed on. He reached the Darling, followed it down about 300 miles to the

Mitchell's party attacked.

site of Menindee, and had to admit that its general course suggested Sturt was right. The natives were troublesome and eventually several, including a woman and child, were killed in an unfortunate affray. Fearing reprisals Mitchell gave up and returned to Sydney.

In March 1836 he left on a third expedition with a very well-equipped party of twenty-four men. Governor Bourke's instructions were that he was first to settle the Darling question by rejoining it at Menindee and following wherever it led. If it did join the Murray he was to follow the latter upstream, with liberty to explore the country to the south if he thought it worthwhile. Mitchell obeyed these instructions only to the extent that they suited himself.

He began by tracing the Lachlan down, rather pointlessly, to its junction with the Murrumbidgee. By this time he had been joined by several natives – Piper, who stayed with him throughout; two named Tommy, who were identified as Tommy-came-first and Tommy-came-last; and a young woman, Turandury, with a daughter, Ballandella, aged about four.

In obedience of orders Mitchell should have headed west across country from the Lachlan to the Darling. Instead he followed Sturt's route down the Murrumbidgee and Murray to where the Darling joined the latter. From there his correct course would have been to trace the Darling upstream to Menindee and so complete its survey, but instead he agreed grudgingly that Sturt was right and left it at that. Again there had been clashes with the Aborigines, in one of which at least seven were shot. Mitchell claimed that these natives included some from Menindee, who had come 200 miles or more to avenge the affair there. If this were true, which seems doubtful, his reluctance to return to the Menindee area is understandable.

After crossing to the south bank of the Murray, Mitchell followed it upstream to the site of Swan Hill. Here he left it

Friendly native woman and her child.

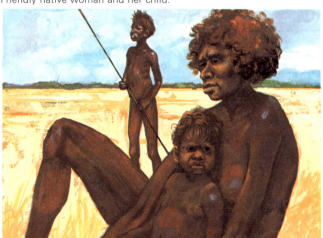

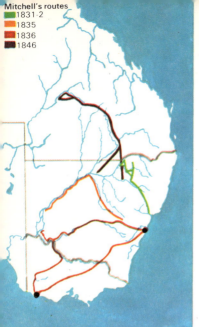

Mitchell's exploration routes and his pistol.

and struck south-west through what is now central and western Victoria. The rich land he found inspired rhapsodical descriptions in his journal, and he called it Australia Felix. He crossed many rivers including the Loddon, Avoca, Avon and Wimmera and eventually reached one flowing south which he named the Glenelg, and which he followed down to its mouth in Discovery Bay, near the present border of South Australia. From here he chose a north-east route homewards which would bring him to the Hume near where Hume and Hovell had crossed it twelve years earlier.

Soon after the party had set out, however, Mitchell was astounded to find a thriving establishment on the coast at Portland, run by the brothers Edward and Frank Henty. During an overnight stay he learned that the Hentys had been there two years, that they were still bringing sheep and cattle across the strait from Van Diemen's Land as fast as ships could carry them, and that they had already built up a profitable trade with whalers in the area.

Mitchell was soon to learn that the Hentys were not the

only unauthorized occupants of country he had thought to be undiscovered. From the summit of Mount Macedon, named by himself, he looked towards Port Phillip, forty miles away, and saw 'a mass of white objects which might have been tents or vessels'. He did not stop to investigate, but in fact he had been forestalled again for what he had seen were the tents, pitched on the present site of Melbourne, of other settlers who had crossed from Van Diemen's Land and were already depasturing at least 30,000 sheep in the area.

More rich country was found on the way home. A member of the party was drowned while swimming a horse across the Broken River at the site of Benalla; and after crossing the Hume, Turandury said farewell and joined King Joey, a Murrumbidgee chief, leaving her daughter with Mitchell. Mitchell had grown fond of Ballandella and took her to Sydney to join his own children. Her eventual fate is unknown.

In Sydney Mitchell received a hero's welcome. Certainly the expedition had been a success. Huge areas of some of the

Mitchell's surprise meeting with the Henty brothers.

Governor Darling.

best land in Australia had been discovered, and the fact that in any case it would soon have been found by squatters pushing north-west from Port Phillip in no way detracts from Mitchell's achievement.

Not all the exploration and expansion had been by land. In 1818 Captain P. P. King, a son of the former governor, had surveyed much of the north coast of Australia and had recommended Port Essington as a suitable base for trade with the East Indies. Six years later Captain J. Bremer was sent there in HMS *Tamar* with troops and convict volunteers, but chose instead a site on Melville Island which he called Fort Dundas. So many people died from tropical diseases or were killed by Aborigines or Malayan pirates that in 1827 Governor Darling sent Captain James Stirling to found a second settlement at Raffles Bay on the mainland. This was also a failure, and in 1829 both were abandoned. In 1826 the appearance of the ship *Astrolabe* in Australian waters had revived suspicion of French intentions, and Governor Darling hurriedly ordered convict settlements to be formed at Westernport, which was still confused with Corio Bay, and at Albany, King George's Sound. Because of its unsuitability Westernport was soon abandoned, and in 1831 the convicts at Albany were withdrawn and it became a free settlement.

Early settlement at Albany, King George's Sound.

A sealing gang at Westernport in the 1820s.

New colonies

Although much of the coast of what is now Western Australia had been discovered and charted by the Dutch two centuries earlier Albany was, in fact, the first white settlement there.

In 1827, less than a year after this remote outpost had been established, Captain James Stirling in HMS *Success*, visited and examined the Swan River area, about 300 miles to the north, on the suggestion of Governor Darling, who visualized it as a possible site for settlement.

Left: Captain James Stirling, whose exploration of the Swan River (below) led to the settlement of Western Australia.

Like Vlamingh, its first discoverer, Stirling was deeply impressed. He took back an enthusiastic report to Sydney, and with Darling's warm support he returned to England and strongly urged that a new colony, free of the taint of convictism, should be formed there. The reaction of the government was mixed. On the one hand there was the question of the cost that would be involved; on the other there was a lingering fear of the intentions of the French. Even if the western half of the continent was no great, glittering prize it was unthinkable that it should be settled by another power, and a usually hostile one at that. This argument won the day. Accordingly Captain Charles Fremantle was sent from the Cape of Good Hope in HMS *Challenger*, and on 2 May 1829 on the site of the port that now bears his name he formally claimed all the continent west of New South Wales for Britain.

To save spending too much money on the new colony the government negotiated to grant large land concessions to a

Ceremony at the foundation of Perth, W.A.

group of investors headed by Thomas Peel, a nephew of the statesman Robert Peel. The syndicate asked for 4,000,000 acres at a nominal price of 1/6 an acre, and in return undertook to settle 10,000 people at the Swan River, to send out 1,000 head of horned stock, to find the settlers in provisions and other necessities, and to establish communication between the new settlement and Sydney. The government countered by offering 1,000,000 acres. This was not acceptable to the syndicate, which withdrew. However, Peel agreed to go ahead on the government's terms, and the project was launched. Stirling was appointed lieutenant-governor and given a small official staff. The first colonists reached the Swan River in June 1829, and settled temporarily at Fremantle while Stirling looked about for a worthy site for the colony's new capital. He found it at last about ten miles upstream, and on 12 August it was officially founded when Stirling's young wife symbolically felled a tree and was given the name of Perth as a tribute to the secretary for the colonies, Sir George Murray, who represented that city in the House of Commons.

Peel was a visionary rather than a practical administrator. When it came to the point he was unable to fulfil all the government's conditions; and this, combined with the

Left: the early settlement of Fremantle from the Canning Road. The entrance to the Swan River is on the right, and Arthur's Head looks out towards the Ocean.
Below: an old windmill at Perth, which is now a museum.

inexperience of many of his settlers made the colony's teething troubles long and painful. Much poor land was interspersed with the good, so that holdings became widely scattered through roadless country, and the settlers had little contact with each other or with Perth. There was no convict labour, free labour was hard to obtain and expensive, and many settlers found the task of clearing their land almost impossible. The colony produced barely enough to feed itself, and even if there had been an export surplus there would have been no market for it. In addition the Aborigines were numerous and

aggressive. After several white men had been murdered Stirling decided he must take firm action against them, and in October 1834 there was an armed clash between natives and a punitive party of twenty-four soldiers, police and civilians near the present town of Pinjarra. One white man was killed and one injured, and estimates of native casualties varied from fifteen to fifty.

Many disillusioned settlers left for the east or returned home, and as adverse reports continued to reach England enthusiasm there quickly

William Buckley
J. P. Fawkner and John Batman.

Batman examines the site of modern Melbourne.

waned. Immigration tailed off and within a few years practically ceased. In 1830 the colony's population was 1800; nine years later it had increased to only 2,150. However, Stirling determined that the colony should not fail; and in spite of everything some progress was made. Perth and Fremantle developed into permanent townships, and smaller settlements were created at Guildford, York, Augusta and the Vasse. The convicts were removed from Albany and it became part of the colony. Further tracts of good land were found and made available to settlers at minimum prices. A weekly newspaper and a bank were founded in Perth and the exportation began of wool and other products. The struggle was long and hard, but by the time Stirling left Western Australia in 1839 the worst was over.

There were no such problems in the east. During the 1820s a flow of free immigrants and capital plus a large reserve of convict labour had brought remarkable prosperity to Van

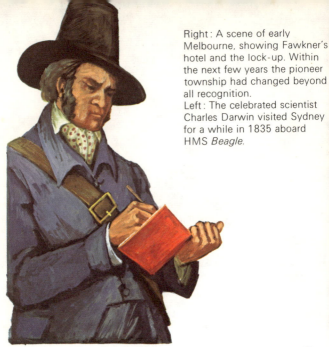

Right: A scene of early Melbourne, showing Fawkner's hotel and the lock-up. Within the next few years the pioneer township had changed beyond all recognition.
Left: The celebrated scientist Charles Darwin visited Sydney for a while in 1835 aboard HMS *Beagle*.

Diemen's Land, and as land became scarcer many pastoralists began to look across Bass Strait for new grazing country, despite the fact that there was a ban on unauthorised settlement there.

In 1835 John Batman, who had won fame by capturing Matthew Brady, a notorious bushranger, crossed to Port Phillip with a small party and chose land near the mouth of the River Yarra as an excellent site for a village. He made friendly contact with the natives and 'bought' from them 600,000 acres of land for the price of a few axes and blankets and some flour. Back in Van Diemen's Land he formed the Port Phillip Association to exploit this obviously illegal deal. In his absence Batman's party rescued William Buckley, an absconder from Collins's original expedition, who had lived with the Aborigines for thirty-two years – a huge, bearded figure in kangaroo skins, who had so completely forgotten his English that it took him months to relearn it.

In the meantime a rival group headed by John Pascoe

Fawkner, a Launceston publican and ex-convict, had also moved in after examining and rejecting Westernport. Before the end of the year Fawkner's and Batman's parties were both established on the Yarra as wary and rather distrustful neighbours, and it was their tents and ships which Mitchell saw from the top of Mount Macedon.

The lure of good land there for the taking was irresistible, and the influx of settlers and stock from Van Diemen's Land continued unabated. Soon cottages and huts began to give the embryo town an air of permanence, and squatters began to fan out west and north-west. By now word of what was going on had reached Governor Bourke in Sydney. As he was bound to do he repudiated Batman's deal with the natives, but wisely made no attempt to eject the unauthorised colonists. Instead he brought law and order to the new settlement by sending Captain William Lonsdale there as resident magistrate, with a small staff of officials.

In March 1837 Bourke himself visited the place, which he named after Lord Melbourne, the British prime minister. On his orders a township was laid out on a rectangular grid pattern. A first sale of allotments took place in June and prices ranged from £18 to £35. At a second sale in November the top price of £100 was paid by Batman for an allotment on the north-west corner of Flinders and Swanston Streets.

The first sale of land at Melbourne.

Progress continued to be rapid. On 1 January 1838 Fawkner published the first newspaper, the *Melbourne Advertiser,* and next day a horseman left for Sydney with the first fortnightly overland mail. By this time squatters had already begun moving in from north of the Murray, and the heavily-rutted tracks left by the carts of Mitchell's expedition did dual duty as a travelling stock route and as a convenient boundary between sheep-runs. In Melbourne stores, hotels and houses were proliferating. Forty-five miles to the south-west another settlement known by its native name of Geelong was also thriving to such a degree that in November 1838 it was proclaimed a town. Fawkner, a shrewd business man who rarely let an opportunity pass, was already on his way to making a fortune. Disabled by illness, Batman was unable to keep pace with his rival, and when he died in May 1839 his financial affairs were already in a confused state.

By the end of 1840 almost all Mitchell's Australia Felix was occupied, and almost a million stock, mostly sheep, were grazing there. The population of Port Phillip district was about 10,000, of whom about 4,000 lived in Melbourne. Lonsdale had been succeeded as superintendent by Charles

Joseph La Trobe, a man of culture and charm, and agitation had already begun for separation from New South Wales.

This desire for independence was heightened by the fact that most of the district's rapidly-increasing revenue was being diverted to Sydney and by a fear that at any time the place would become a dumping ground for convicts; and feeling grew so intense that in 1841 a deputation was sent to England to urge that Port Phillip be given free colonial status. In the same year Bourke's successor Sir George Gipps visited Melbourne; and by the end of it the district's population had doubled to 20,000, due mainly to the arrival of almost 8,000 free immigrants.

In 1842, as a step towards self-government, the Legislative Council of New South Wales was enlarged by the addition of twenty-four elected members, and Port Phillip was allotted six of these seats. The practical effect was not great, for as the Council met in Sydney these six members had to be Sydney residents. Nevertheless, Port Phillip now had at least some small voice in its own affairs.

The first settlement at Geelong in the 1830s

By the end of the year the boom was over, and in common
with the rest of Australia Port Phillip was suffering a serious
economic depression. Wool prices, which had been falling
steadily, reached a disastrous level, and sheep sold for as little
as 6d each. Many pastoralists who had borrowed heavily
to build up their flocks had no money coming in to pay off
their debts, and in a year more than a hundred went bankrupt.

There was a gradual return to prosperity in the next few
years. Surplus sheep were slaughtered and boiled down for
tallow, which sold profitably. Pastoralists began to manage
their properties more economically, and recovery was further
aided by a fall in the cost of living and an increase in the price
of wool. With a return to normal the demand for separation
became even more vociferous. The people of Melbourne
deliberately sabotaged an election of 1848 by returning Earl

86

Grey, the Secretary of State for the Colonies, as their representative; and a year later when two transports turned up in Melbourne with about 500 convicts the irate citizens threatened to prevent their landing by force and insisted on their diversion to Sydney.

By now almost every acre of Mitchell's Australia Felix was occupied, and the district had 6,000,000 sheep and a human population of 70,000. Obviously separation could be delayed no longer, and it was granted by the British government in August 1850. The new colony was officially named Victoria, and La Trobe was appointed its first governor. When the news reached Melbourne three months later the town celebrated for a fortnight, with bands, processions, fireworks, balls and public meetings. Prayers of thanksgiving were offered in all the churches, and publicans made a small fortune.

Left: Collins Street, Melbourne, in 1839.
Below: Charles La Trobe and his cottage at Joliment. La Trobe, who arrived from England in 1839, was the first superintendent of Port Phillip and later the first lieutenant-governor of Victoria.

Colonel William Light and early Adelaide, S.A.

Meanwhile, to the west of Victoria another colony had come into being. In England there had been much pondering over the failure of the Peel scheme in Western Australia; and in 1829 a pamphlet appeared called *A Letter from Sydney*, which outlined an ideal theory of colonization. Although it was published anonymously its author was soon identified as Edward Gibbon Wakefield, who was in Newgate prison for having abducted a fifteen-year-old heiress and marrying her at Gretna Green. Wakefield argued that if a new colony were concentrated, Crown lands could be readily sold at a fairly high price and the proceeds devoted to bringing out labourers and their families, who would then save and buy land further out, thus providing more money to bring out more immigrants, who in turn would save their wages and buy land still further out until the whole colony was occupied.

It was a plausible theory, and though it took little account of realities it won many disciples in England. South Australia, which had not yet been settled, seemed a good spot to try out Wakefield's ideas, and eventually a South Australian Association was formed with George Fife Angas, a London banker and shipowner, as its leading spirit. The government passed a South Australian Act which vaguely divided control between the Colonial Office and the company, and by the end of 1836 more than 300 settlers had arrived in the new colony.

From the start there were clashes between the governor, Captain John Hindmarsh, and the government surveyor, Colonel William Light, regarding the most suitable site for a capital which was to be called Adelaide after King William IV's queen. Light was the winner and Adelaide was duly founded a few miles in from the coast on a river named after Colonel Robert Torrens, the company's chief representative in the colony.

Equally serious quarrels soon arose between Hindmarsh and Torrens. Hindmarsh wanted to be free to select the best land, irrespective of where it was situated; Torrens stuck

The landing place at Port Adelaide.

rigidly to Wakefield's plan of concentrated settlement. The folly of divided control soon became apparent in England. The Wakefield theory was abandoned as impracticable, Hindmarsh was recalled, and his successor, Colonel George Gawler, was given full authority to run the colony as governor and commissioner. One result was that the South Australian Association went bankrupt.

There had been little agricultural development during this period, and when Gawler arrived Adelaide was in the grip of a land boom, with town allotments fetching up to £10,000. Goods of all kinds were scarce. Stock overlanded from New South Wales was bringing inflated prices and a few speculators were making fortunes importing food and other necessities. Although the boom soon collapsed people continued to arrive, and by 1841 the population had reached 14,000. Among the newcomers were many Germans, frugal and hard-

Immigrants on their way to South Australia.

The German village of Klemsig, near Adelaide.

working, who formed their own villages at Klemsig and Bethany and retained many of their own customs.

Gawler tried to create jobs by embarking on a big scheme of public works, but the British government was shocked by the size of the bills that began to pour in, and in 1841 he was replaced by Captain George Grey, who had already won some fame as an explorer. Grey's arrival coincided with the country-wide economic depression, and the position in South Australia went from bad to worse. Grey's rigid economies, although probably necessary, were widely unpopular. Unemployment

and insolvencies soared, and many people were forced out of Adelaide to make a living as best they could from the land. One result was that by 1843 the colony was producing more wheat than it could eat. This largely solved the food problem but did little more, for freight and insurance charges were too high for the surplus to be exported at a profit.

By 1844 Grey had balanced the colony's budget. Admirable as this feat may have been it was the discovery of valuable minerals, however, which finally pulled the colony out of its depressed state. Silver-lead had been found at Glen Osmond near Adelaide in 1841 and copper at Kapunda, forty miles away, in the following year. But both these were spectacularly surpassed in 1845 by rich finds of copper at Burra Burra. In five years the Burra Burra mine yielded £750,000, investors who had all but ruined themselves in the collapse of the land boom had recouped their losses, and the recently-stagnant colony was enjoying a prosperity it had not known before.

Left: Ben Boyd's yacht, *Wanderer*.
Below left: Rich copper finds at Kapunda ended the financial depression in South Australia.
Below: Rundle Street, Adelaide, in the late 1840s.

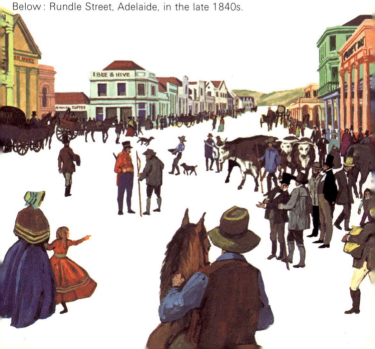

Explorer George Grey threatened by natives.

Opening the inland

By 1835 explorers had revealed much of the face of eastern
Australia. But much unknown country remained, particularly
in Queensland, western New South Wales, and the mountains
of the far south-east. In the new colonies of South and Western
Australia geographical knowledge extended little beyond the
settled areas, and almost all northern Australia was still a
blank. There were many theories regarding the unknown
inland. Some believed the centre to be one vast desert; others,
like Sturt, still thought it might contain an inland sea.

In 1836 Lieutenant George Grey, the future governor of
South Australia, won official support for an expedition in
Western Australia. A year later he and a small party, only
one of whom had been in Australia before, were landed
at Hanover Bay, on the north-west coast, with the ambitious

94

idea of travelling overland to Perth, about 1,500 miles away. They were soon in trouble, in rugged country among hostile natives. Grey, who had already narrowly escaped drowning, was severely wounded by a spear, and with great difficulty the party found its way back to the ship. Even so, Grey had discovered a river flowing through fertile valleys which he called the Glenelg. He had also found some cave-paintings, the origin of which continued to be a mystery until the twentieth century.

Grey tried again in 1839. He and eleven others set off from Perth and were landed in three whaleboats near Shark Bay, meaning to work their way down the coast and land from time to time to explore the inland. Once more the plan miscarried. All three boats were destroyed in heavy seas, and the party had no choice but to walk 500 miles back to Perth. One died on the way and others arrived in pitiable condition. The one positive result was the discovery of several rivers and a large tract of good country inland from the present town of Geraldton.

In the south-east corner of

Strange rock and cave paintings found by Grey near the Glenelg River, W.A.

95

Explorer Eyre saved by a French whaling ship.

the continent a year later Count Paul Strzelecki discovered
Australia's highest peak and named it Mount Kosciusko after
a Polish patriot. Continuing south he and his party struggled
through thickly-timbered mountainous country, sometimes
progressing a mere couple of miles a day. Horses and supplies
had to be abandoned and the party reached Melbourne
exhausted and half-starved. Strzelecki called the area he had
discovered Gippsland.

Meanwhile in South Australia Edward John Eyre, who
had been a pioneer in overlanding stock to Adelaide, had
tried twice, in 1839 and 1840, to reach the centre of the
continent, but had been thwarted each time by the immense
dry salt bed of Lake Torrens and by lack of water.

In 1841 Eyre was beaten yet again, but instead of returning to Adelaide he sent most of his party back and set
off from Fowler's Bay with only one white companion, John
Baxter, and three Aborigines to reach Albany in the west. It
was an appalling journey of almost 1,000 miles around the

head of the Great Australian Bight, mostly through treeless, waterless desert. Baxter was murdered by two of the Aborigines, who plundered the stores and ran away. Only a chance meeting with a French whaler at Rossiter Bay saved Eyre and the third native, Wylie, from death by starvation and enabled them to reach Albany, a further 300 miles away. The heroic journey, which had taken nineteen weeks, achieved little beyond proving what Eyre had already guessed – that no practical stock-route existed between the east and west.

Mount Kosciusko

Eyre and the faithful Wylie reach Albany.

Port Essing

Drysdale R.

Dat

Vict

Fitzroy R.

Great Sandy
Desert

De Grey R.

Fortescue R.

Hamersley Range

Macdonnell Ra

Ashburton R.

Gibson Desert

Gascoyne R.

Shark Bay

Murchison R.

Great Victoria Desert

Nullarbor Plain

Swan R.

Perth

Great Australia

Blackwood R.

Albany

	Grey
	Eyre
	Strzelecki
	Sturt (3rd journey)
	Leichhardt
	Mitchell (4th journey)
	Kennedy

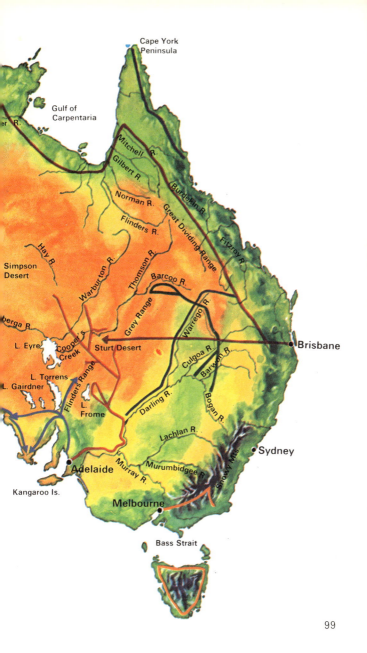

Cape York
Peninsula

Gulf of
Carpentaria

ar R.

Mitchell R.

Gilbert R.

Norman R.

Burdekin R.

Flinders R.

Great Dividing Range

Fitzroy R.

Hay R.

Simpson
Desert

Warburton R.

Thomson R.

Barcoo R.

berga R.

L. Eyre

Cooper's
Creek

Grey Range

Warrego R.

Sturt Desert

Brisbane

L. Torrens

Culgoa R.

Barwon R.

L. Gairdner

Flinders Range

L.
Frome

Darling R.

Bogan R.

Lachlan R.

Adelaide

Murray R.

Murrumbidgee R.

Snowy Mts.

Sydney

Kangaroo Is.

Melbourne

Bass Strait

99

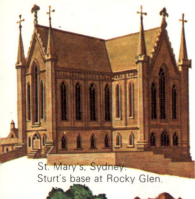

St. Mary's, Sydney.
Sturt's base at Rocky Glen.

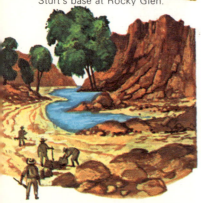

In 1844 Charles Sturt, who had been for some years a public servant in Adelaide, entered the field again. With a well-equipped party of fifteen he followed the Darling River up to Menindee, the place of such bitter memories for his rival Mitchell, and then struck out north-west in an attempt to reach the centre of the continent.

On his way Sturt crossed the Barrier Range near the site of Broken Hill, and after a harassing journey through dry desert country he found permanent water at a spot he called Depot Glen, near present Milparinka. He meant

Explorer Sturt defeated by the Great Stony Desert.

to rest there only briefly but in fact was forced to remain almost six months through a drought-stricken summer so unbearably hot that, as he recorded, 'horn handles and combs were split into fine laminae, the lead dropped out of our pencils, our hair ceased to grow, and our nails became as brittle as glass'. Heavy rain brought relief at last. But it also brought tragedy for a few days later Sturt's second-in-command, John Poole, died of scurvy.

To eke out provisions Sturt sent some of his people back to Adelaide and pressed forward with the rest. A new depot was established at Fort Grey, and from here Sturt made several probing journeys towards the centre, but was defeated each time by an almost impassable stony desert which still bears his name. Sturt's own health broke down at last, and he was forced to give up. To survive the return journey through waterless country he had four bullocks killed and their hides made into water casks each holding about 150 gallons, and the party travelled mostly by night. Sturt was now too ill to ride and had to be carried in a dray. Although he recovered well he was still weak when he reached Adelaide, and recorded that his wife fainted at first sight of him.

While Sturt was trying vainly to reach the centre another expedition was making its way north-west from Brisbane towards Port Essington on the north coast, a journey of about 2,000 miles through unknown country. It was privately financed and led by an eccentric German, Ludwig Leichhardt, who had left Prussia to avoid military service. Leichhardt had an almost mystic faith in his own genius as an explorer, but he was a poor bushman and no leader. Two of his party resigned and returned to Brisbane; and a third, John Gilbert, an ornithologist, was killed and two others were seriously wounded in a night attack by Aborigines. However, Leichhardt pressed on, and after an appalling journey of more than fourteen months he and his companions staggered half-dead into Port Essington.

In Sydney Leichhardt had long been given up for dead, and on his return he was hailed as a hero. He gave lectures and wrote a book, and he received handsome cash awards from the government and private citizens. In December 1846 he set out from the Darling Downs to cross the continent over-

Port Essington, the goal of Ludwig Leichhardt.

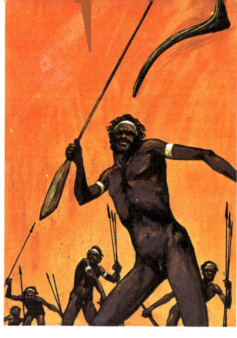

Above: a caricature of Leichhardt.
Right: natives of Carpentaria launching an attack on his party.

land to Perth, but bad weather, illness and constant quarrels with some of his party forced him to return without having achieved anything. Undeterred, Leichhardt left once more in April 1848, with Perth again his objective. Neither he nor any of his six companions, of whom two were Aborigines, were ever heard of again.

In the meantime Major Mitchell had set out with a strong and well-found party of thirty-two on what was to be his last expedition. His object this time was to find a practical overland route between the settled districts of New South Wales and the north coast of the continent. His dream of the mythical Kindur had died hard, and he still hoped he would find a large river which he could follow to his goal.

The journey, although uneventful, was certainly fruitful. Beyond the present Queensland border Mitchell found the rich and extensive Maranoa plains and much more good grazing land, which today is the heart of the Queensland cattle country. Further north he received what he called 'a reward direct from Heaven' when he came upon a wide river flowing north-west which he named the Victoria. He was sure this was the stream he had so long sought, but as food supplies were low he was unable to follow it down, and he and his party returned to Sydney.

Early in 1847 Mitchell's second-in-command, Edmund Kennedy, was sent with a small party to trace the course of this river; and Mitchell's confident belief that he had made a major discovery was shattered when Kennedy returned with the deflating news that the true course of the river was

Left: the survey ship HMS *Rattlesnake* in New Guinea waters. Below: the tragic death of Edmund Kennedy in the jungle country of Cape York. Jacky Jacky is fighting off the attackers.

south-west, and that it was in fact merely the upper part of Cooper's Creek, called by the natives the Barcoo.

The following year Kennedy left Sydney again, this time with twelve companions, to explore Cape York peninsula. The barque *Tam o' Shanter* took them to Rockingham Bay, south of present Cairns, from whence they were to make their way overland to the tip of Cape York, where the schooner *Ariel* would meet them.

From the start they were hampered by thick jungle and harassed by hostile natives. Vital food supplies were lost and the balance had to be strictly rationed. Eight of the party became so weak that Kennedy left them at Weymouth Bay, about 150 miles short of their objective, and pushed ahead with the remaining four, who included an Aborigine named Jacky Jacky. One accidentally shot himself and another became too ill to continue, so Kennedy left the three white men at Shelburne Bay, about seventy miles from the Cape, and he and Jacky Jacky continued on alone. They fell in with savage natives who dogged them for several days and then attacked. Kennedy was speared in the back and right side and died soon afterwards. Now alone, Jacky Jacky eventually reached the *Ariel* which sailed at once to rescue the others. No trace could be found of the three who had been left at Shelburne Bay, and of the eight who had remained at Weymouth Bay only two survived.

Newchums and squatters

In the early days there had been little to entice settlers to Australia. When Governor Macquarie left in 1821 it was still essentially a penal colony, with convicts greatly outnumbering free inhabitants and most of its wealth was concentrated in the hands of a few 'exclusives'. Its potentialities, however, were by then becoming obvious enough. Fine wool from John Macarthur's Merino flocks was bringing up to 10/- lb. in England and good breeding rams were worth £200 each. It seemed clear that the country's future lay in wool, and with the discovery almost every year of vast tracts of good pastoral land more and more Englishmen were tempted to seek their fortunes in the new country. Many of the 14,000 free immigrants who arrived in the 1820s were men of capital, ambitious and willing to work hard. They included practical farmers, skilled artisans, doctors, lawyers, army and navy officers and university graduates. Many were the younger sons of aristocratic families who hoped to find the opportunities in Australia that were denied them at home. Whatever their background, however, they were lumped together in colonial eyes as 'newchums'. Some lacked the ability to come to terms with their strange and harsh environment and either drifted futilely as remittance men or returned

Below: squatters measuring out a sheep run.
Above right: immigrants going ashore in Sydney.
Right: a coach being guided across a flooded river.

home. But others adapted surprisingly well, and among the pioneers who pushed inland with their flocks and herds in the wake of the explorers were many men of this type. Even so not all had the resilience to survive the discomforts and hazards of outback life, and many were forced to give up under the onslaught of droughts, floods, bushfires and the depradations of 'duffers' (stock thieves), bushrangers and hostile natives. But for those who stuck it out there were rich rewards, and from them and their children eventually arose the privileged class which became known as the 'squattocracy'.

Technically the occupation of Crown land beyond the limits of settlement was illegal, and in 1829 Governor Darling proclaimed a settled area of nineteen counties, stretching from the present Taree on the north coast of New South Wales to Moruya in the south and westward to Wellington, Orange and Cowra, and ruled that nobody should go beyond these. But as a later governor, Sir George Gipps, pointed out it was as impossible to keep the squatters within defined bounds as to 'attempt to confine an Arab within a circle traced on the sand', and equally impossible to prosecute them for trespass.

In 1831 the practice of making free land grants to favoured immigrants was discontinued after almost 4,000,000 acres had been disposed of in this way. The minimum price of Crown land was fixed at 5/- an acre, increased to 12/- in 1838 and to £1 in 1842, and squatters beyond the settled areas were obliged to pay a grazing licence based not on the actual number of stock they owned but on the carrying

Below: night attack on a store dray.
Above right: squatters in their first home. After the gold discoveries successful squatters built imposing houses.
Right: police resist an attack.

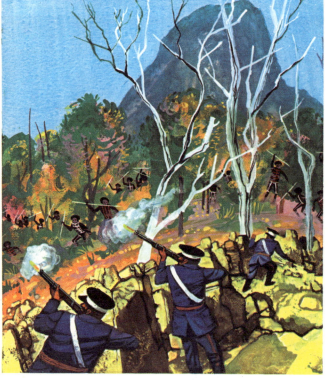

capacity of their runs. The income from land sales was used to subsidize immigration on what was known as the bounty system. Between 1831 and 1840, as a result, more than 65,000 free settlers arrived, and as convicts became outnumbered, the whole social structure of the colonies underwent a profound change.

On the whole the squatters were against this mass immigration of free settlers, among whom were many yeomen farmers, as a potential threat to themselves; whereas they still welcomed convicts for the cheap labour they provided. Among the rest of the community, however, there was a growing feeling that the convict system was basically bad and that Australia could only hope to progress as a land of free men.

Convict-powered tramway near Port Arthur.

A rest-break for convict workers in Van Diemen's Land.

Enlightened opinion in England supported this attitude, and in 1840 transportation was abolished except to Van Diemen's Land and Norfolk Island. For awhile it was replaced by a new system, under which good-conduct prisoners in English jails were sent out as 'exiles' and given their freedom when they arrived on condition that they remained in the colonies until their sentences had expired. But this created such a storm of protest in Australia that it was soon discontinued. By a strange irony Western Australia, which had begun proudly as a free colony, was now so desperately short of labour that it was the only one which would accept convicts. But even there it was eventually found that the evil outweighed the good, and in 1868 the last British convicts were landed on Australian soil.

In the meantime the eastern colonies had won some measure of self-rule by the addition of elected members to the various Legislative Councils. Many of these elected members were wealthy squatters or their business associates and the result in New South Wales, which at that time still included the Port Phillip district, was a bitter struggle between the squatters and Governor Gipps, who believed in a fair

The old homestead and the new, exemplifying the rise of a pioneer squatter to affluence.
Right: Governor Gipps in a wealthy squatter's home.

distribution of land and firmly resisted their claims to privileged treatment. One of the chief complaints of the squatters was that they had no security of tenure of the vast areas they occupied. Another was that by abolishing the convict assignment system Gipps forced them to employ free labour at high wages; and feeling on these and other issues became so strong that there was even talk of armed rebellion.

In addition to his fight with the squatters Gipps had to cope with the general economic depression of the 1840s. Although revenue from land sales had practically ceased, immigrants continued to pour in at a rate of thousands a year, and Gipps had to introduce rigid economies to save many of them from destitution and the colony itself from bankruptcy.

As a result he became widely unpopular, and the squatters were by no means alone in celebrating when he resigned and returned to England. Yet Gipps spoke the truth when he wrote: 'I have laboured to the best of my ability to advance the true interests of this land'. Today it is agreed that he was one of Australia's ablest governors.

The squatters' fight for power continued undiminished for many years after his departure. By the late 1850s all the colonies except Western Australia were self-governing, and it was apparent that something would have to be done to straighten out the hopelessly confused and inadequate land laws. In particular, there was strong agitation to break up the large sheep and cattle runs, because it was felt that much grazing land could be more profitably exploited growing wheat and other crops or in intensive dairy farming; and various acts were passed with this in view.

In most colonies these worked well enough, but in New South Wales they created chaos. Without a preliminary survey, selectors were given the right to buy holdings of up to 320 acres at £1 an acre on easy terms, on condition only that they effected improvements to a value of £1 an acre within three years; and the rush for land created much bitterness between the squatters and the 'cockies', as the small farmers became known. Some selectors bought merely

The first train from Sydney to Parramatta receives a rousing reception on its arrival.
Below: SS *Chusan*, the first mail steamer to Australia; and a selector's hut.

for speculation; others hoped that by acquiring key areas –
near water, for instance – they could force the squatters to
buy them out at inflated prices. Many of the squatters,
equally unscrupulous, bought large areas of the best of their
own leasehold land through dummies and indulged in
'peacocking', or acquiring areas that denied the selectors
access to water. At times the conflict became almost as fierce
as that between ranchers and homesteaders in the American
west. The squatters destroyed fences and allowed their stock
to trample down growing crops, and selectors stole or killed
the squatters' sheep and cattle. Destructive bushfires were
deliberately started and there were instances of actual
physical violence. The situation went from bad to worse,
and a committee which investigated the scheme condemned
it as 'opening the door for every phase of abuse and fraud'.
In the end the squatters won an almost complete victory, and
it was not until the present century that equitable land laws
were introduced.

Hargraves and the Turon River diggings

The gold rush

It was neither the discoveries of the explorers nor the growth of the wool industry that revolutionized Australia and paved the way for nationhood. It was gold.

Convicts building the Blue Mountains road in 1815 are said to have found traces of gold near the site of Bathurst. Certainly James McBrien, a government surveyor, did so in the same area only eight years later and reported the fact to Governor Brisbane. Among others who found gold west of the Blue Mountains were Count Strzelecki, the explorer, at Hartley in 1839, and Reverend W. B. Clarke, an amateur geologist, near Hassan's Walls in 1841. In the next few years several more finds were reported, particularly by shepherds in New South Wales and Victoria, but they were small and created little interest.

Many thousands of Australians were lured across the Pacific in the great Californian gold-rush of 1849. In the same year a man named Smith showed a lump of gold quartz to officials in Sydney and offered to reveal its source if suitably rewarded; but Governor FitzRoy suspected the gold came from California and the offer was rejected.

Australia's gold era really began with the return from California in January 1851 of Edward Hammon Hargraves, a man of formidable physical bulk and something of a braggart. Although unsuccessful in America Hargraves had shrewdly noted the similarity between the gold-bearing country there and in the region of Bathurst, where he had had a small sheep run. On his return he went with a youth named Lister to Summer Hill Creek, which he had known well, and on 12 February, according to his own story, the first pan he washed of creek soil yielded gold. Back in Sydney Hargraves not only officially reported his find in expectation of a reward – eventually he was to receive £10,000 – but boasted of it to friends. The news quickly spread. By April some hundreds of diggers were on the spot, which soon grew to

Gold-diggers paying their licence fees.

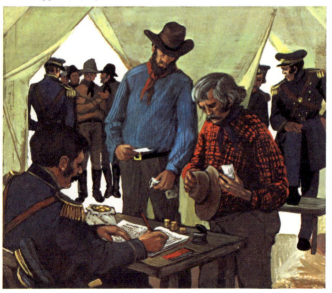

become the town of Ophir. Within a month or so much richer gold was found at Sofala on the Turon River, and when word reached Sydney the rush was on in earnest.

Some diggers made quick fortunes. Others barely managed to pay their way. The weather was bitter, conditions were primitive, the work was hard and food and other goods, which had to be hauled from Sydney, were scarce and expensive. FitzRoy sent commissioners and police to administer the fields, and every digger was obliged to pay a licence fee of 30/- a month.

The lure of gold denuded Sydney of most of its male population, and soon thousands of fortune-seekers were flocking in from the other colonies. The exodus from Victoria in particular created such a labour shortage that wealthy employers combined to offer a large reward for the discovery of gold within 200 miles of Melbourne. There were several immediate claimants, but the man who found the first really payable field was James Esmond, known as 'Happy', who by coincidence had returned from California in the same ship as

Hargraves. Esmond's discovery was at Clunes, ninety-seven miles north-west of Melbourne. Within weeks prospecting parties nearby at Buninyong and Ballarat and further north at Bendigo and Mount Alexander had made such fabulous finds that in the first six months gold worth more than £1,000,000 had been won.

In Melbourne shops and offices closed, lawyers deserted their clients and doctors their patients. Building and other works came to a stop, government departments were reduced to skeleton staffs, and so few police were left that neighbours banded together for mutual protection. Soon gold-seekers were flooding in from England and America. As they stepped ashore they were joined by seamen and officers, and the port became cluttered with deserted ships. Wages and prices soared, and with accommodation impossible to obtain a sprawling tent-town arose on the banks of the Yarra. Tents and humpies, offering accommodation and sly-grog, lined the muddied road to the diggings. Bushrangers robbed and sometimes murdered and not only isolated travellers but

Gold escort attacked by bushrangers.

Eureka Stockade. Troops storming the diggers' flimsy barricade.

even armed gold-escorts were held up. Most diggers earned little more than their wages, but fortunes were made as well, sometimes in a week or even a day. Some of the lucky ones were prudent. Others gambled away their gains or spent them on champagne and high living. Men lit their pipes with £5 notes or ate them in sandwiches. In 1852 alone Victoria's population soared from 77,000 to 172,000. By the end of 1854 it had more than doubled again, and gold worth £10,000,000 a year was being won.

Charles Joseph La Trobe, who had become the first governor of Victoria, was far too gentle a man to cope with

Memorial on the site to the men who fell at Eureka.

such a revolution. To meet the immense cost of maintain
ing law and order he imposed the same licensing system a
in New South Wales. The diggers accepted it for awhile,
then rumbles of discontent grew to a roar and mass meetings
of protest were held throughout the diggings. The fee
itself was bad enough, but the mode of collecting it worse.
Digger-hunting became a favourite sport among the troopers,
many of whom were young 'bloods' recently arrived from
England; and as they galloped through the diggings in search
of prey it needed only hunting horns and packs of hounds to
make the illusion complete.

By mid-1854 La Trobe had given up, derided by the diggers
and abused by the newspapers, and had thankfully handed
over to his successor Sir Charles Hotham. Hotham, due for
promotion to rear-admiral, tried to run the colony as though
it were a battleship, and of course he failed. Ballarat, by now
easily the richest and most populous of the fields, was also
the centre of the diggers' unrest. The violent death of one of

them and the acquittal of his murderer by a corrupt magistrate
set off a train of events with which Hotham's quarter-deck
methods were totally unable to cope. As troops marched in
to Ballarat to maintain law and order, so the anger of the
diggers mounted.

Yet another digger-hunt, even more humiliating than most
was the final straw. Led by Peter Lalor, son of an Irish M.P.
the diggers burned their licences, swore an oath of loyalty
built a flimsy stockade at Eureka, and raised their own flag
a Southern Cross on a blue ground. Instead of negotiating
Hotham chose to meet the challenge with force. Before dawn
on 3 December 1854 troops and armed police took the stockade
by storm, and when it was over about thirty men were dead
It was in every way a pointless affair, for Hotham had already
decided to appoint a commission to investigate conditions on
the goldfields, and had this been known bloodshed might
have been avoided. Within another few months almost all
the diggers' grievances had been redressed, and by the end
of 1855 Hotham himself was dead of overwork and strain
the last victim of his own stiff-necked inflexibility.

By 1856 the roaring days were all but over. Most of the

surface and near-surface gold had gone, and it took capital to sink the deep shafts to recover what remained. Companies took over, and individual miners worked for them or went back to their old occupations or returned home. Ballarat grew into a solid and staid Victorian city.

The increasing number of Chinese on the various fields soon posed a new problem. In Victoria alone there were more than 40,000 of them. They were hard-working and frugal, content to scratch a living from the tailings discarded by earlier diggers, and their presence became a source of

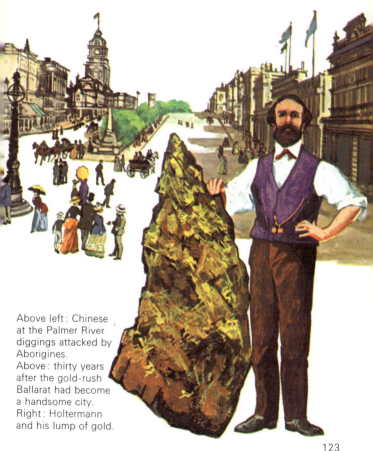

Above left: Chinese at the Palmer River diggings attacked by Aborigines.
Above: thirty years after the gold-rush Ballarat had become a handsome city.
Right: Holtermann and his lump of gold.

123

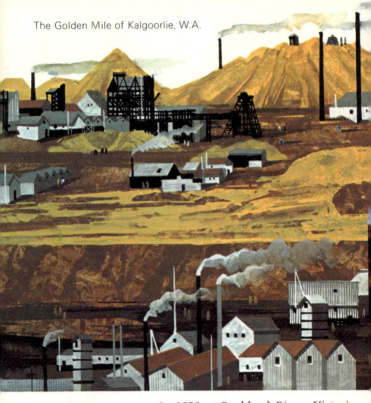

The Golden Mile of Kalgoorlie, W.A.

mounting resentment. In 1858 at Buckland River, Victoria, and two years later at Lambing Flat, New South Wales, there were riots in which their camps were destroyed and many Chinese injured.

In 1870 rich gold finds at Gulgong and Hill End, in the same general area as the old Bathurst fields, caused a new rush. By 1872 there were 30,000 people in Hill End alone, and in the same year a lucky digger unearthed the largest single mass of gold ever known, weighing 630 lb and worth £12,000.

The main rushes in Queensland were at Canoona (1857), Mount Gympie (1867), Charters Towers (1872) the Palmer River (1872) and Mount Morgan (1882). Some boom towns had a brief life, but reef gold is still being produced at Mount Morgan. As in the south a big influx of Chinese led to several

riots, particularly at the Palmer River, and eventually Queensland followed the lead of the other colonies by passing laws
which severely restricted their entry.

The last great rush occurred in Western Australia in 1893,
when Paddy Hannan made a rich strike at what is now
Kalgoorlie, about 350 miles inland from Perth. Fortune-
seekers poured in from all over Australia, and production
soon exceeded 1,000,000 oz. a year. A railway was built to
link the field with Perth, a pipeline was added to bring water
to the parched area, and there was no lack of English capital
to finance deep-sinking. At its peak in the early 1900s the
Golden Mile, as it became known, was yielding gold worth
up to £10,000,000 a year, and many mines in the area are
still working profitably.

The dead heart

Although the first great gold rush had distracted public attention from exploration men soon began again to wonder what lay in the unknown inland.

There had been strange rumours that the explorer Leichhardt had been captured and was being held by a band of escaped convicts who had formed a settlement somewhere in the interior; and although these were generally disbelieved it was felt that some attempt should be made to find traces of the missing German. With this in view Augustus Gregory, who had done some minor exploring in Western Australia, left Sydney by sea in July 1855. He and his party were landed near the mouth of the Victoria River, on the north coast, and after following this down they penetrated about 300 miles south-west before desert country forced them back.

Stampede of horses at Gregory's camp.

McDouall Stuart reaches the centre of Australia.

They then turned east, following in reverse Leichhardt's route to Port Essington, and in four months reached the Queensland coast near Rockhampton.

In 1858 Gregory made a second search for Leichhardt. This time his route took him from the Maranoa country discovered by Mitchell through central Queensland. He followed the Barcoo River down until it became Cooper's Creek, and then travelled almost due south to Adelaide. Although he found no trace of Leichhardt, Gregory did much to dispel the idea that the centre of the continent was entirely desert.

During 1858 and 1859 John McDouall Stuart, who had been with Sturt on his final expedition, made two deep probing journeys northward from Adelaide, and in 1860 he set off again with a small party hoping to cross the continent from south to north. On his journey Stuart discovered the fertile

Burke and Wills on their dash to Carpentaria.

MacDonnell Ranges near the site of Alice Springs, and on a hilltop at the geographical centre he built a cairn and raised the British flag. In tribute to his old leader he called this Mount Sturt, but today it is known more fittingly as Central Mount Stuart. Within 400 miles of his objective Stuart had to turn back for home, defeated by spinifex desert, hostile natives and scurvy among his men.

Meanwhile a much more elaborate cross-continental expedition was being organized in Melbourne, led by Robert O'Hara Burke, a police officer without exploring experience, who is said to have undertaken the task to impress Julia Matthews, an actress. Burke and his party of seventeen, with twenty-five camels imported from India, left Melbourne in August 1860 and travelled slowly to Menindee. By this time his deputy, George Landells, had resigned after a quarrel and William John Wills, the party's astronomical observer, was promoted in his place.

From Menindee Burke, Wills and six others pushed on to

Cooper's Creek and formed a forward depot. For six weeks Burke waited impatiently for the rest of the party. Then, he determined as he wrote to 'cross the continent at all hazard', a distance of 600 miles each way through mostly unknown country. Four men were left at the depot with orders to remain three months, and Burke set off with Wills, John King, Charles Gray, six camels, a horse and twelve weeks' provisions.

In March 1861 they reached tidal waters in the Gulf of Carpentaria but were unable to reach the open sea because of mangrove swamps. Their three months were up and provisions were low. Gray, who had been whipped for stealing food, died on the desperate journey back; and when the others reached Cooper's Creek depot they learned that the the rest of the party had left only seven hours earlier for Menindee. Instead of following they decided to make south for Mount Hopeless and thence on to Adelaide. For awhile they wandered, exhausted and starving; then Wills died, followed two

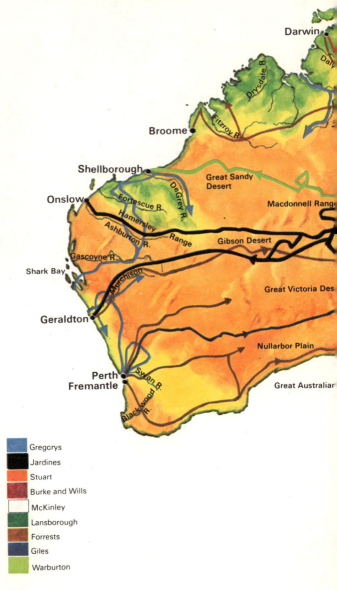

Darwin

Broome

Shellborough

Onslow

Shark Bay

Geraldton

Perth
Fremantle

Drysdale R.

Daly

Fitzroy R.

Great Sandy
Desert

Macdonnell Range

Fortescue R.

De Grey R.

Hamersley
Range

Ashburton R.

Gascoyne R.

Murchison

Gibson Desert

Great Victoria Des

Nullarbor Plain

Swan R.

Blackwood R.

Great Australian

Gregorys
Jardines
Stuart
Burke and Wills
McKinley
Lansborough
Forrests
Giles
Warburton

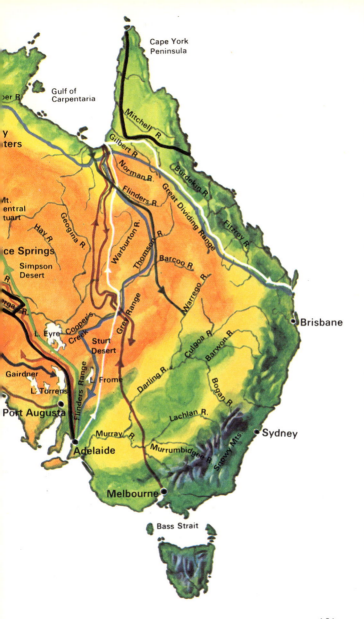

Cape York
Peninsula

Gulf of
Carpentaria

er R.

y
ters

Mitchell R.

Gilbert R.

Norman R.

Burdekin R.

Great Dividing Range

Mt.
entral
tuart

Flinders R.

Geogina R.

Hay R.

Warburton R.

Thomson R.

Fitzroy R.

ce Springs

Simpson
Desert

Barcoo R.

Warrego R.

Brisbane

Grey Range

L. Eyre

Cooper's
Creek

Sturt
Desert

Culgoa R.

Barwon R.

Gairdner

Flinders Range

L. Frome

Darling R.

Bogan R.

L. Torrens

Port Augusta

Lachlan R.

Sydney

Adelaide

Murray R.

Murrumbidgee R.

Snowy Mts.

Melbourne

Bass Strait

days later by Burke. King survived precariously on native roots and fish given to him occasionally by the local Aborigines, and when eventually found by a relief party from Melbourne led by W. A. Howitt he was in a pitiable condition, almost a walking skeleton.

Howitt's was only one of four expeditions which were sent to look for Burke and Wills. A second, led by John McKinlay, headed north-east from Adelaide; a third, with William Lansborough in charge, was put ashore in the Gulf of Carpentaria and worked its way south, and a fourth, under Frederick Walker, travelled west from Rockhampton. Walker found the tracks of the missing explorers and followed them for some distance, and McKinlay recovered the body of Gray. However, the real importance of these expeditions was that all three revealed the existence in the Queensland interior of big areas of rich, well-watered grazing country.

Meanwhile, undeterred by earlier failures and rapidly failing health, McDouall Stuart was still determined to reach

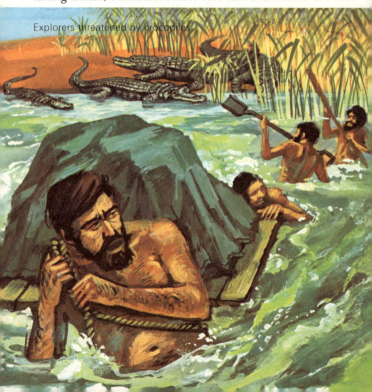

Explorers threatened by crocodiles

Stuart completes his crossing of the continent.

he north coast from Adelaide. Early in 1861 with government backing and a well-equipped party he followed his earlier track north, only to be thwarted by apparently impenetrable scrub within 300 miles of his goal. Later in the same year he tried yet again. From Newcastle Waters, his furthest point on the previous expedition, he made several probing journeys in various directions until eventually he broke through the scrub near Daley Waters. From here he pushed resolutely on to the headwaters of the Adelaide River, and a week later, on 24 July 1862, his exhausted but jubilant party reached the sea not far from the site of Darwin. The journey home was a long ordeal. Many of their horses died, the party were harassed by natives, and for a time Stuart was paralysed and blind and had to be carried in a litter slung between two horses. They returned to a heroes' welcome in Adelaide. 'All the married ladies assembled made a rush at me, and for five minutes I was nearly smothered', one wrote later. 'Talk about the charge of the Light Brigade; 'twas nothing to the charge these ladies made.' Completely shattered in health from his

Leaders of the overland telegraph construction party.

six expeditions Stuart returned to England, where he died in June 1866, aged only forty-one.

As a result of Stuart's successful crossing, settlements were established within the next few years at the mouth of the Adelaide River and at Port Darwin, which was first called Palmerston; and in 1870 the South Australian government voted £120,000 for an overland telegraph line from Adelaide to Darwin to link with a submarine cable from Java and so open direct communication with England. The chosen route, which mainly followed Stuart's track, totalled 1,973 miles.

Ayers Rock, central Australia, which its discoverer called 'the biggest pebble in the world'.

through largely uninhabited country. It was divided into southern, central and northern sections, and work on all three began simultaneously. Despite many difficulties and hardships the job was completed in less than two years, and on 21 October 1872 the first direct cable message from London was received in Adelaide. There were public banquets in Sydney, Adelaide and London, and the South Australian postmaster-general, Charles Todd, who had had overall charge, was knighted for his epic achievement.

At intervals of about 200 miles along the line maintenance and relay stations were built and staffed, with the result that explorers were given fixed starting and finishing points which greatly reduced the dangers of their journeys.

The first to take advantage of this was Ernest Giles, who left the line at the Finke River in August 1872 hoping to reach the west coast. However, his way was soon blocked by the impassable salt bed of Lake Amadeus and he was forced to give up. In April 1873 Major Peter Warburton set out from Alice Springs, also bound for the west coast, and quickly found himself in the midst of a vast waterless desert. Most of his party became ill and camels had to be killed for food. Nevertheless they pressed on travelling mainly at night, 'fleeing as it were for our lives', so Warburton wrote, and most were near death from exhaustion and starvation when the coast was reached near Roeburne. In the same year Giles was defeated again, this time by the Gibson Desert; and the same formidable barrier drove back W. C. Gosse, who had set out from Alice Springs only a week after Warburton.

In 1874 John and Alexander Forrest, brothers who were already highly reputed as explorers, left the port of Geraldton to cross the interior from west to east. At Weld Springs, with about a third of the way covered, they had to beat off an attack by natives. Thirst was an even more implacable enemy as they crossed the Gibson Desert, and on one occasion only a providential fall of rain saved their lives. The last stretch was slow and arduous, and when they reached the telegraph line in November 1874 they had been on the track more than seven months.

The indefatigable Giles was on the job again in 1875 when

Above : Giles and his party attacked by natives.

Below : Forrest reaches the telegraph line from W.A.

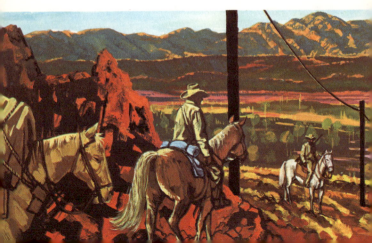

he made a successful east–west crossing from Beltana, on the telegraph line, to Perth, in the course of which he passed near the site of Kalgoorlie; and in the following year he crossed west–east from Geraldton to Oodnadatta on a route to the north of that of the Forrests.

Although these heroic journeys filled many huge blanks on the map, their only practical effect was to prove that much of the West Australian inland was uninhabitable desert; and it was left to Alexander Forrest in 1879 to discover a great tract of first-class cattle land in the Fitzroy, Ord and Victoria River areas in the far north-west.

Sir John Forrest.

Last of the bushrangers

One effect of the long and bitter struggle between squatters and selectors was a fresh outbreak of bushranging in New South Wales and Victoria, which began in 1861. Unlike the old school, who were mainly convict escapees or thugs tempted by the rich rewards of the gold rush days, the new generation were free-born youths and young men, often the sons of small farmers, who had grown up with a reckless contempt for authority in general and for their natural enemies, the squatters, in particular.

The first to achieve notoriety was Frank Gardiner, a twice-convicted horse thief, whose field extended from Bathurst to Yass. Gardiner's first partner, John Piesley, was soon caught and hanged, but there was no lack of recruits to replace him. In June 1862 Gardiner and his gang, which included Johnny Gilbert, a young Canadian, stuck up a gold escort at

'Bail up!' The order that coach passengers came to dread in the bushranging days of the 1860s.

'Brave' Ben Hall, in life and death.

Eugowra Rocks near Forbes and got away with £12,000 in gold and notes. Gardiner then disappeared and his place as leader was taken by Ben Hall, who some say was driven to crime by police persecution. For nearly three years Hall, Gilbert and their followers ranged the country, robbing banks, lone travellers, mail coaches, station homesteads, and once even kidnapping a magistrate and holding him to ransom. In a gun duel in 1863 Gilbert shot dead a police sergeant named Parry; and soon afterwards another of the gang, John Dunn, shot and killed Constable Nelson at Collector, a village near Lake George. In 1864 Gardiner was tracked to Queensland, where he was running a store and hotel. He was sentenced to thirty-two years' hard labour, but was released after eight on condition that he left the country. He died in the United States about 1895. Meanwhile, Hall, Gilbert and Dunn had been declared outlaws, to be shot on sight. In May 1865 Hall was ambushed by police and killed, and a week later Gilbert suffered the same fate. It is said that both were betrayed. Dunn escaped at the time but was caught some months later and was hanged in March 1866.

Further south people in the Monaro and Riverina districts were being terrorized by 'Black Dan' Morgan, a lone operator noted for his brutality. In 1865, with a price of £1,000 on his head, Morgan crossed into Victoria, where for awhile he robbed travellers, plundered homesteads, shot cattle and burned haystacks. His career ended abruptly when he made a typical night raid on a homestead. A nursemaid managed to send a message for help, and next morning as Morgan was about to mount his horse he was ambushed and shot dead.

In northern New South Wales the most notorious bush-ranger at this time was an escaped prisoner, Frederick Ward, who called himself 'Captain Thunderbolt'. Like Morgan, Ward usually worked alone, but there the similarity ended for Ward prided himself on his courtesy to his victims and his gallantry to women. For a long time his hardships were shared by his half-caste wife, but she eventually died of tuberculosis. Her loss deeply affected Ward, and soon afterwards he was shot

Last stand of Captain Moonlite's youthful gang.

dead in a duel with a policeman near the town of Uralla, N.S.W.

Another remarkable figure was Andrew George Scott, alias 'Captain Moonlite', the son of an Irish clergyman and himself a lay preacher. One night in May 1869 a masked man held up a bank at Bacchus Marsh, Victoria, where Scott worked as a clerk, and got away with about £1,000. The manager swore the man was Scott, but his story was disbelieved and he was himself arrested and charged. However, Scott was caught soon afterwards with some of the proceeds of the robbery and was sent to jail. Good conduct earned him an early release in 1879, and for a time he returned to itinerant preaching. Then for no apparent reason he gathered together a gang of five youths and began a bushranging career. He and his gang were cornered at Wantabadgery, near Wagga Wagga, and in a pitched battle two of them and a policeman were shot dead. At the trial of the survivors Scott accepted the blame, and as a result two of his followers escaped with

Black Dan Morgan, worst of the bushrangers, showed mercy to none.

Hero or hoodlum? The last stand of Ned Kelly at Glenrowan.
Right: An unglamourized police picture of Kelly and the armour
he fashioned from ploughshares.

prison sentences. Scott himself and one other were hanged.

The best-known of all Australia's outlaws was, however, Ned Kelly. His father, a former convict, died while Kelly was still young, and during his teens Kelly and others of the family were often in trouble for horse-stealing; but it was not until his mother was sent to jail on what seems to have been perjured evidence that Kelly decided on an active bushranging career. With a younger brother, Dan, and two friends, Joe Byrne and Steve Hart, he went into hiding in wild mountain country in northern Victoria, and when police tracked them down Kelly shot and killed three of them. As a result all four were declared outlaws.

This massacre was followed in December 1878 by the daring robbery of a bank at Euroa, which involved holding a large number of people as hostages at a homestead a few miles out of the town. Two months later the gang crossed the border to Jerilderie, N.S.W., locked the town's two policemen in

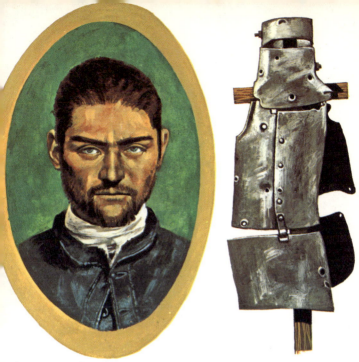

their own cells, plundered its only bank at leisure, and got away with £2,140. After lying low for another year they emerged again. Byrne shot and killed an informer named Aaron Sherritt, and next day the gang took over the village of Glenrowan and detained most of its population in the local hotel. A plan by Kelly to wreck a special police train misfired, and instead the hotel was surrounded by armed police and an all-night siege took place. Byrne was killed by a stray bullet, and about dawn Ned Kelly emerged in a suit of armour made from ploughshares, apparently determined to fight it out alone. Police brought him down by firing at his unprotected legs, and he was captured. Later that day the hotel was fired, and in its charred ruins were found the bodies of Dan Kelly and Hart, who had apparently committed suicide. Four months later Ned Kelly was tried and hanged, and with his death Australia's last and most spectacular bushranging era came to an end.

The Duke of York opens the first Federal Parliament.

Australia discovers herself

By the 1880s the heroic age of exploration was over, and only small isolated pockets of the continent still remained unknown. Now that their country had been discovered it was time for the Australians to discover themselves. It was to be a slow and often tedious and painful process, and it is not over yet.

At this time there was little sense of national identity, and people tended to think of themselves as, for instance, Victorians or New South Welshmen rather than as Australians. Politically the country still comprised six entirely separate self-governing colonies, which owed more allegiance to Great Britain than to each other. Each ran its own transport and communications, its own armed forces such as they were, its own education and medical and postal systems. Customs tariffs, taxation, land and industrial legislation, and immigration and foreign policies differed greatly and often conflicted. Several intercolonial conferences had been held in an attempt to achieve some sort of unity, but all had failed because of considerable mutual supicion and jealousy.

Commonsense dictated that if eventual chaos were to be averted some form of federation was essential, and in 1889 the Premier of N.S.W., Sir Henry Parkes, came out strongly in favour of this. At a series of intercolonial conferences many problems were discussed and settled in principle, a constitution was drafted and debated and revised, and it seemed that federation was just around the corner. But Parkes was old and ill, and when he died in 1896 it seemed his cause might die with him. However, the occasion brought forth the man – Edmund Barton, a barrister and superb orator. Campaigning up and down the country Barton won over the waverers, and on 1 January 1901 the Commonwealth of Australia was proclaimed with Barton as its first Prime Minister. For awhile it made little difference to the man in the street. The colonies were now called states, and there was a federal parliament, which sat in Melbourne. Defence, postal services, foreign policy, tariffs and a few other things had

Parkes, Father of Federation.

Barton, Australia's first P.M.

Bushmen off to the Boer War.

The sinking of the German raider *Emden*.

been unified, but for the rest life went on very much as it had before.

The Edwardian years were pleasant and prosperous. There were occasional rumbles from Europe, and in 1910 Lord Kitchener arrived to advise on Australia's defences. But potential trouble seemed far away and remote; and in any case what country would dare challenge the might of Great Britain's navy? But Germany did dare; and when, on the outbreak of war, Prime Minister Fisher announced that

Australian attack on Achi Baba, Gallipoli.

Prime Minister Hughes.

Britain would be supported 'to our last man and our last shilling' he spoke for virtually the whole country. If any particular date is to be assigned to Australia's birth as a nation, it is 4 August 1914.

By November a large force of Australian and New Zealand volunteers was on its way to Egypt. Off Cocos Island the light cruiser *Sydney* left the convoy to destroy the German raider *Emden*, but otherwise the voyage was uneventful. The Anzacs, as they became known, were to complete their battle training in Egypt and then transfer to France. Instead, Britain decided to attack Turkey through the Dardanelles to ensure a Mediterranean Sea link with Russia. The landing at Gallipoli in 25 April 1915, was spearheaded by Anzac troops, but the Turks had been forewarned and were in strength. There were weeks of ferocious fighting and weeks of stalemate before the Allied commanders admitted defeat. In January 1916 the last troops were withdrawn from the futile campaign which had cost Australia 8,500 dead and 19,000 wounded.

For the rest of the war the Anzacs fought in France against the Germans and in Palestine against the Turks. Many names of these campaigns – Bapaume, Bullecourt, Messines, Ypres, Passchendaele, Villers Bretonneux, Mont St Quentin, Beersheba, Damascus – still have a ring of glory. On 11 November 1918, when the German armistice was signed, of the 330,000

The first Qantas passenger plane.

Native stretcher-bearers in New Guinea.

Australian volunteers who fought overseas almost 60,000 had been killed and 166,000 wounded.

In the post-war years Australia grew up fast, stimulated by a boom. Large estates were broken up and servicemen were settled on the land. Subsidies encouraged primary producers and tariffs encouraged manufacturers. By the autumn of 1929 the world was drifting into economic depression which hit hard at Australia. As conditions improved elsewhere, by 1932 the depression in Australia was over, and somehow adversity had acted to draw the people closer together and unify them still more as a nation. When war came again in 1939, it seemed for a while to follow the pattern of the earlier one. Anzacs were sent to Palestine to train for the western front, but by June 1940 the German panzers had swept through western Europe and there was no western front. Instead the Anzacs fought in the north African desert, at

Bardia, Tobruk, Derna and Benghazi, first against the Italians and then against the Germans. Across the Mediterranean they suffered heavily in retreats from Greece and Crete.

The war became global in December 1941 when Japanese dive-bombers devastated an American fleet at Pearl Harbour. Three days later the myth of Britain's naval might was shattered when two of her battleships were sunk off Malaya. By mid-February 1942 Singapore had fallen, the survivors of a whole Australian division were in Japanese hands, and as the enemy swept south, Australia herself was in imminent danger of invasion. Darwin and Broome were bombed; midget submarines even penetrated Sydney harbour. In a courageous statement Prime Minister Curtin said that Australia could no longer look to Britain for help and that only the United States could save her. Under the command of General Douglas MacArthur an American fleet and American troops and aircraft and supplies poured in. Civilian Australia went on to a complete wartime footing. By now the Japanese, advancing irresistibly, were in New Guinea and the Solomons. Then the situation changed dramatically with two great naval victories by the Americans in the Coral Sea and off Midway Island. Slowly the tide turned. The enemy was checked and

Australian assault troops go ashore under fire.

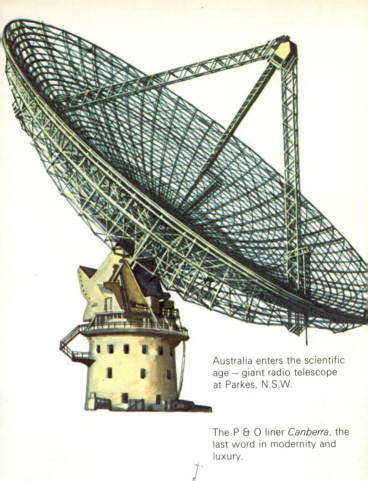

Australia enters the scientific age — giant radio telescope at Parkes, N.S.W.

The P & O liner *Canberra*, the last word in modernity and luxury.

A remarkable Australian
invention — the Jindivik pilotless
target plane.

One of several underground
power stations that are part of
the Snowy Mountains complex.

The Academy of Science at
Canberra, Australia's national
capital.

Open-cut uranium mine at Rum Jungle, Northern Territory.

steadily pushed back. New Guinea was freed; and one after another the Japanese were flushed bloodily from their island strongholds. In May 1945 the war in Europe was over. Ten weeks later atomic bombs obliterated Hiroshima and Nagasaki, and the Pacific war was over too.

Australians emerged from the holocaust united as never before. They were one people, one nation. Sentimental ties with the home country remained, but they knew they could never again rely on Britain's protection. It was clear that their natural ally in the Pacific was the United States. It was clear too that for Australians Europe was no longer the centre of the world, and that their future depended on relations with their neighbours in south-east Asia. Since 1945 Australian foreign policy has been based almost completely on these two simple propositions. She was a founder of the South Pacific Commission (1947) and of the Colombo Plan (1950). In the same year, 1950, she signed the Anzus Pact, a mutual defence treaty with the United States and New Zealand. In 1953 she was one of eight founder-members of SEATO, the South-East Asia Treaty Organisation, which is devoted to deterring Red Chinese aggression by a policy of mutual economic, technical and cultural aid; and in 1966 she was a founder of ASPAC (Asian and Pacific Co-operation Council).

New political and economic alliances alone were not enough, however, and Australia's most urgent needs were to expand industrially and to develop her immense natural resources. To accomplish these goals she needed people. Since the war more than 2,000,000 migrants, mostly government-assisted, have settled in Australia. A majority are British, but they come from many countries, particularly from Greece, Italy and Yugoslavia. Assimilation has proved no great problem. In twenty-one years to 1968 Australia's population increased from 7,500,000 to 12,000,000; in another twenty-one it may total 20,000,000.

Cities such as Sydney and Melbourne have expanded beyond all recognition. Australia's population is now overwhelmingly urban, and today's manufacturing output would have seemed unthinkable twenty years ago. Yet primary production has not declined; and the vast areas over which explorers toiled and often died a mere century ago are now producing another kind of wealth. Mineral finds are so frequent that it is impossible yet to assess the country's reserves of lead, zinc, mineral sands, iron ore, bauxite,

Sydney Cove, less than 200 years after its settlement.

The Australian flag.
National Gallery and Arts Centre, Melbourne.

manganese ore, silver, tin and tungsten. To these must be added extensive recent discoveries of nickel, phosphate rock, oil and natural gas. Imported oil once cost Australia £150,000,000 a year. By 1980, the experts say, she will be self-sufficient.

In these exciting post-war years Australians have grown greatly in self-confidence and maturity of outlook. They no longer inhabit a remote colonial outpost. Jet aircraft have brought the whole world within easy reach. The old sense of isolation, of dependence on a far-off motherland, has died, and with it the old sense of inferiority. Few Australians nowadays have chips on their shoulders. They don't need to. Their living standards are among the highest in the world. Unemployment hardly exists. Their industrial arbitration system, although not perfect, is far in advance of those of most other countries. They have rejected socialism for a virile democracy, and they have shown that it works. Their philo-

154

sophy of a fair day's work for a fair day's pay is reflected in the country's exceptional rate of productivity growth.

In other than material ways there has been great development too. Universities are proliferating; educational standards have never been higher. Among intellectuals there is an increasing trend to take a long hard look at Australia and where it is heading. Some dislike quite a few things that they see, and they say so. The books they write, far from being resented, are often best-sellers. For a nation once hypersensitive to criticism this is a healthy sign. In all the arts a recognisably Australian school is emerging. It is no longer enough for painters, for instance, to paint well. Their work must express something peculiarly and particularly Australian, and a surprising amount of it does. The same is true of creative writing, of music, of the theatre and ballet. Sydney makes jokes about her Opera House, but she is proud of it too, as Melbourne is proud of her new Arts Centre and Adelaide of her Arts Festival.

With Australia on the crest of such a gigantic wave no-one can be quite sure yet exactly where she is heading. But even her severest critics, those who call her 'the lucky country', are proud of her and believe implicitly in her future. So does every Australian today.

Sydney's spectacular opera house.

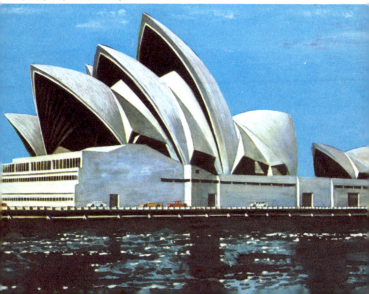

FURTHER READING

Shaw, A. G. L. and Nicholson, H. D. – *Growth and Development in Australia* (Sydney, 1966)

Shaw, A. G. L. and Nicholson, H. D. – *Australia in the Twentieth Century* (Sydney, 1967)

Pike, Douglas – *The Quiet Continent* (Cambridge, 1962)

Fitzpatrick, Kathleen (Ed.) – *Australian Explorers, a selection from their Writings* (London, 1958)

Roberts, S. H. – *The Squatting Age in Australia* (Melbourne, 1964)

Blainey, Geoffrey – *The Rush that Never Ended* (Melbourne, 1963)

INDEX

Page numbers in bold type refer to
illustrations

SOME OTHER TITLES IN THIS SERIES